Praise for *The Executioner's Redemption*

The Executioner's Redemption: My Story of Violence, Death, and Saving Grace is the most exciting book about a Christian's experience I have read. The story of his life and the powerful message he is delivering is so compelling it was difficult to take a break, even for sleep.

This book is about how God desires all of us to walk with Him and to grow in our understanding of His plan for our life on earth. Tim has shown through this book exactly how we can apply God's Word to our everyday activities. While Pastor Tim uses his criminal justice experience to give us understanding of Satan's unceasing attack, he provides practical methods for us to use the power of the Holy Spirit to blunt Satan's best efforts.

Every sentence, every paragraph, and every page lays forth the pure theology of God's Word. This story speaks to the prison guard, the police officer, all criminal justice practitioners, every judge and jury member, and to every Christian. I truly regret I didn't have the benefit of this book to help keep me grounded during my thirty-seven-year career as a police officer and manager of police service in the fourth largest city in the United States. I highly recommend this book to everyone.

—Jerry W. DeFoor
Assistant Chief of Police (Retired)
Houston Police Department
Houston, Texas

This book, in part, reflects the transformational journey from a nonpracticing Christian to a self-righteous and judgmental one, and then to a man willing to die-to-self, allowing others to see Christ live through him. In the past six years, Rev. Carter has helped me personally go beyond the carnal, judgmental attitude of dealing with criminals. I believe I have learned from him to look through the lens of grace, inwardly knowing that we all are fallen and are in need of God's redemption and help. Rev. Carter serves as an example of the power of Christ, who can take someone from an empty path of self-fulfillment to a path of trusting in God and being fulfilled completely so that it is evident to all that meet you.

—Sergeant James D. Rhoads
Houston Police Department

A riveting must-read that I could not put down! From hard-hearted executioner to God's gentle servant, Tim Carter's incredible journey of self-discovery and perseverance powerfully illustrates that no one is beyond God's life-changing transformation. Tim's experience on the Texas death squad vividly proves that God's peace and love shine brightest in the darkest places. This book will inspire you, make you gasp, cry, and laugh. It beautifully morphs hope into fact that with God ALL things are possible.

— *Donna Pyle*
Speaker, Bible Teacher,
and Author of Quenched: Christ's Living
Water for a Thirsty Soul *(CPH 2014)*

The Executioner's Redemption shows how our God can mold and shape someone's life through His Word even in the hardest of circumstances. I was blessed to know Captain Carter during some of the hardest years of my life. In my teen years I began to let the enemy take control and lusted for every evil thing imaginable. I ended up in prison at age 27, and the Holy Spirit used Tim Carter's witness to impact my life. Now, as a Christian, I have continued to keep in touch with Rev. Carter, and he has continued to inspire and shape my life each and every time I talk to him.

— *Donald Tapley*

While a friend of Tim Carter for years, I never really knew him until reading *The Executioner's Redemption*. This is an intriguing story of Tim's journey from prison guard to prison death squad to ordained Lutheran pastor.

In addition to gripping stories of prisoners he encountered, Tim addresses the perennial question of capital punishment, sharing his own personal struggle in a compelling biblical exegesis of the balance between God's mercy and God's justice. His dual role as penitentiary administrator and ordained pastor catapults Tim Carter into the rarified company of another friend, the sainted Dr. George J. Beto, and makes this book a fascinating read!

— *Rev. Dr. Gerald B. (Jerry) Kieschnick*
President Emeritus | The Lutheran Church—Missouri Synod

The Executioner's Redemption
My Story of Violence, Death, and Saving Grace

REV. TIMOTHY R. CARTER

Published by Concordia Publishing House
3558 S. Jefferson Ave., St. Louis, MO 63118-3968
1-800-325-3040 • www.cph.org

This book recounts events in the life of Timothy R. Carter according to the author's recollection and from the author's perspective. The events and experiences detailed herein are true and have been faithfully rendered as remembered by the author, to the best of his ability, or as told to the author by people who were present. Some names, identities, and circumstances have been changed to protect the privacy, anonymity, and or integrity of individuals involved.

Library of Congress Cataloging-in-Publication Data
Names: Carter, Timothy R.
Title: The Executioner's Redemption / Timothy R. Carter.
Description: St. Louis : Concordia Publishing House, 2016.
Identifiers: LCCN 2015029632 | ISBN 9780758652591
Subjects: LCSH: Death--Religious aspects--Christianity. | Death row. |
   Life--Religious aspects--Christianity.
Classification: LCC BT825 .C388 2016 | DDC 261.8/3366--dc23 LC record available at http://lccn.loc.gov/2015029632

1 2 3 4 5 6 7 8 9 10   25 24 23 22 21 20 19 18 17 16

CONTENTS

FOREWORD

Faith in Extremis

About that strange title, *"in extremis,"* —who uses Latin anymore anyway?—I'll explain later. For now, let me welcome you to this book. As you get into Tim Carter's life and jaw-dropping stories, please keep asking yourself, "What do all his experiences mean for my personal faith?"

I was born a year-and-a-half after the end of World War II. America had come through terrible times—the Great Depression and the War—and had come through in triumph. It was a time of great optimism and hope that we youngsters took in with almost every breath. "With work and determination, there's nothing you can't do," the adults taught us. "Why, you could even go to the moon," and we did. But then life came along, and more than a few times those feelings of youthful idealism were knocked out of us, something like a three-hundred-pound tackle taking down a smaller running back. That's aging, and in some ways in contributed to weakening my personal faith.

My brother, sister, and I were raised in a wonderful Christian home—I couldn't have asked God for better. We were taught to attend church every Sunday, went to Sunday School and Christian day school, and knew that this was very important to our parents. Family, church, and school modeled the truth, "God is love" (1 John 4:8). Yes, we learned about sin, but we were kids and America was overtly Christian, at least in appearance if not always in the hearts of all its citizens. But then suffering came along: relationship struggles, family members contending with illnesses not always curable, and of course, visitations at the funeral home for relatives and for our father when he was only in his sixties. Beyond our family, we saw that other people didn't have it as good as we did, like the people "on the other side of the tracks." Where's this God of love? And that, too, impacted my feelings about God and contributed to the weakening of my personal faith.

One more category, though I could add more and you probably could too, having had your own less-than-ideal moments in your relationship with God. We were taught the Ten Commandments, even memorized them. Our parents were interested in all the grades on our report card, but heaven help us if we came home with anything less than A's in religion, memory work, effort, and conduct. Again, we had idealism instilled, spiritual idealism, but as we grew older we saw go-to-church Christians doing things they ought not to do. My father had a saying: "You dasn't do that." It was a kind of German-American expression, I guess. But our feelings about God and faith took a hit when we saw fellow Christians doing things that the heavenly Father had said, "You dasn't do that." "Thou shalt not." Their less-than-A+ conduct was another significant contributor to the weakening of my personal faith.

So what was going on, and in fact still is going on, with my faith? *Every Mother's Nightmare* by Charles Bosworth Jr. describes a horrific crime. Teenager Stacy was babysitting three-year-old Tyler when an intruder forced his way in and brutally murdered both children. I met Stacy's mom, Jude Govreau, when she appeared on a TV program I was hosting, *On Main Street*. The program explored the dimensions and benefits of faith in life. When I asked Jude what that terrible experience did to her faith—I still shudder, years later, as I recall the horror of the crime—she answered, "It took it away." Her answer invites reflection: what exactly is faith? Jude's feeling that faith in God had been taken from her, my experiences over the decades, and Tim Carter's changing relationship to God during his twenty-one years working for the Texas Department of Corrections all turn on an understanding of what faith really is. How your own experiences impact your faith relationship with God is something you'll have to ponder for yourself, but if you do that personal reflection as you read this book, you'll be blessed. So then, what is "faith"?

We naturally equate "faith" with our feelings. So the murder of Stacy took away any positive feelings that Jude had for God, and we certainly can understand her reaction, her loss of "faith." As I described my own reaction to experiences such as aging, suffering, and the conduct of others, things I said "contributed to the weakening of my personal faith," I was careful to write that those experiences impacted my *feelings* about God. You, too, have had experiences that weakened your warm and fuzzy feelings about God. And on almost every page Tim talks about the wide range of feelings he had as he dealt with "human wolves." Feelings about God—that's a part of faith that you'll explore in this book, but only a part.

In the Bible the word *faith* has two aspects. One is our feelings toward God. There's nothing wrong with this. How many of us get teary when we worship on Christmas or Easter? That's our emotions, our feelings, subjective. But in the Bible there is another aspect to faith, and in fact it's even more important than how we're feeling about God. This aspect is objective, not subjective. It is outside of us (external), not within us (internal). This other aspect of faith wasn't born in us, as our feelings are, but this other aspect of faith comes to us from outside, totally from outside of us. This fundamental aspect of faith is the promises of God to us in Jesus Christ. When our feelings toward God are weakened, God's promises to us in Jesus Christ cannot be weakened because they're from God, who never changes and is true to His word.

You can understand the whole Bible as a book of promises. The promises are not all sugar and spice and everything nice. For example, in Ezekiel 18:4 God promises, "The soul who sins shall die." That includes all of us, good religious people and death row inmates. God kept that promise not by sending you to the eternal prison but by sending His Son, Jesus, to suffer the punishment for sin in your place. Jesus said that He came "to give His life as a ransom for many" (Mark 10:45). Again, Jesus promises, "I am the resurrection and the life. Whoever believes in Me, though he die, yet shall he live, and everyone who lives and believes in Me shall never die" (John 11:25–26). That promise of eternal life in heaven is a promise He will keep to you and to everyone who believes Jesus is their Savior, and that includes inmates on death row who turn to the only Savior. There are hundreds more promises in the Bible to instruct, admonish, and encourage us. The Bible tells us that all the promises are centered on Jesus Christ. "For all the promises of God find their Yes in Him" (2 Corinthians 1:20). Tim Carter became a Bible student because he yearned deep in his being to know and hang on to the promises. Indeed, that's the heart of faith, hanging on to the promises, especially when everything is pummeling our good feelings about God. God doesn't change, God doesn't lie, and God doesn't renege on His promises. In His own time, God keeps His word. "If we are faithless, He remains faithful—for He cannot deny Himself" (2 Timothy 2:13).

That's faith. Sometimes our feelings about God are upbeat, warm, and sunny, but other times we feel down on God, cloudy and cold days. Either way, faith is hanging on to God's promises in Jesus Christ. As you turn each page and hear Tim share his own feelings about God in light of Scripture, this dual aspect of the word *faith* will be evident. However, one thing is different about Tim's journey from our own, and the difference is caught in those strange words in the title, "Faith *in Extremis*." Those Latin words mean "in a difficult situation," often "at the point of death." The words are so succinct that you'll see them every now and then in your English reading. Tim's growth in faith came facing death, the death of others. The ultimate questions of good and evil, punishment and forgiveness, love and hate, life and death, God and us . . . All those questions were put inescapably before Tim every day for those twenty-one years. His feelings and trust in the promises of God were forged *in extremis*, in facing the death of others. God led Tim to internalize death, to see that true faith meant his own personal dying, dying to himself and his feelings, to trust instead in the God who wants to save all people. Jesus says, "Whoever would save his life will lose it, but whoever loses his life for My sake and the gospel's will save it" (Mark 8:35).

In these pages you'll be invited to faith *in extremis*, to dying to yourself so that the promises of Christ can fill your life. I have found that to be true, that faith is less about my feelings and more about trusting the promises with all my heart, soul, and mind (Matthew 22:37). I hope that Jude has found it, that she has come to know peace from the promises. And I pray that insight for you as you walk through these pages with Tim. "I have been crucified with Christ. It is no longer I who live, but Christ who lives in me. And the life I now live in the flesh I live by faith in the Son of God, who loved me and gave Himself for me" (Galatians 2:20).

Dale A. Meyer
President, Concordia Seminary

INTRODUCTION

What you are about to read will take you behind the scenes of the physical and emotional world of death row. During my time as a member of the execution squad in the state of Texas, my experiences became "classrooms" through which God taught me what matters most in life. These learning experiences may cause you to be shaken by observations of the most oppressive darkness. Although the circumstances in dealing with death row inmates and the capital punishment process are extreme, I believe that you will relate to many of the dilemmas and find fresh hope and inspiration from my story.

The life lessons I have learned stem from my interactions with death row inmates and other execution participants, all with varying points of view. Many condemned inmates, their families, and anti-capital punishment activists think of the death squad members as merciless, bloodthirsty wolves. Judges and juries of the state of Texas, however, consider virtually everyone they sentenced to death to be the merciless and bloodthirsty ones. These contrasting opinions tugged my heart in different directions and taught me life lessons I couldn't have learned anywhere else.

In the Bible, God often calls His people "sheep" and refers to those who try to physically or spiritually kill them as wolves. The apostle Paul (Saul of Tarsus), before his conversion, was a ravenous wolf who preyed upon God's flock. Penitentiaries are filled with every kind of human wolf imaginable and, like Saul of Tarsus, I was one of them for a season. I became a product of my environment, zealous to do what I mistakenly thought was right, following the wrong mentors into a deep ditch.

As one empowered to wield the "sword of the state," I went through a turbulent pilgrimage of experiences that shaped my heart and soul. Therefore the following story is not simply a gratuitous look inside death row; it is the story of the progression of my faith in Christ—a relationship that triggered a long and serious struggle to know His will concerning my authority and responsibility in wielding that sword. This is also not a treatise for or against capital punishment. It recognizes that the "sword of the state," if misused, can result in grievous harm and at the same time be a God-given restraint of evil.

The lessons revealed in the following pages are unique, yet affect everyone. While only thousands are commissioned to wield the "sword of the state," everyone must support and yield to that authority—be they police, military, or others.

This journey includes a parallel consideration of the sword of the Spirit as it describes my initial exposure to reading and hearing God's Word, followed by a growing appreciation for and eventual dependence on that Word. Some of the life lessons reveal that the sword of the Spirit can be abused in much the same way as the sword of the state. The Word of God can be twisted out of context by people with twisted hearts and minds.

The majority of life lessons stem from my reluctant transformation and failure to align my spirit with the Word of God. This is about my journey to discovering the truth among conflicting influences in a hostile environment. It's about learning that when it comes to dealing with people who choose to live by the sword of violence, there are definite Christian responsibilities for all crime fighters and private citizens.

The human wolves who prey upon others not only diminish their victims, but they also weaken the very fabric of society. We are compelled to carefully consider all of the affected lives so dear to God. Having spent most of my life working for the Texas prison system, particularly with death row inmates, their families, and the families of their victims, I had a unique opportunity to examine all sides of the situation. I saw the deepest darkness of pain and suffering caused by sin and evil in the world. I was also blessed, however, to see the bright light of God's hand at work in the lives of every person affected by the sword of violence and the sword of the Spirit.

Although I studied for many years at Sam Houston State University, earning a degree in criminal justice, I learned far more by praying my way through the heart-rending atrocities of prison life and diligently searching God's Word for wisdom and direction.

This humble volume is about startling life lessons learned while dealing with death row inmates on the last day of their lives. It's about love lessons from those deemed unlovable. It's about heart lessons from God. But mostly it's about God's will for and activity in the lives of wounded sheep and deranged wolves. It is my hope that these pages will inspire those who are empowered to wield the sword of the state, and will bless those whom they serve as well.

Some of the very blunt and stark realities of life deep inside a prison and the capital punishment process may be unnerving and uncomfortable; nevertheless, I encourage you to continue taking this very emotional ride with me. I trust that you will be moved by its destination. I pray that the Lord will hold you tightly if any aspects of this journey might open a personal wound in a victimized heart. My greatest reward for writing this book would be that God would use my experiences, along with the life lessons I learned through them, to help you look to Him for direction through life's most painful and troubling times. To you, to the victims of predatory criminal actions, and to those who dedicate their lives to fighting crime and keeping the peace, you are in my prayers and in God's heart. May the Lord draw you closer to Him through this journey.

CHAPTER 1

Shaped by the Sword of the State

"He really is a good boy," the mother said. I was caught off guard. I had to pause and silently stare at her for a moment, digesting her words. It was the day of her son's execution. I had just finished explaining in detail the rules she was expected to follow when she entered the prison to witness the event. Her thoughts and focus were understandably somewhere else, and it was obvious that she had not heard a single word I had just said.

The lady stood a little over five feet tall. She was dressed respectably sharp, yet casual, had shoulder-length salt-and-pepper hair, and was probably in her late forties. Her demeanor was calm and very polite as her eyes shifted down at the floor, then back up at me, then quickly down to the floor again. She took a deep breath, quietly stared into my eyes for a moment, and with a slight southern drawl, she said, "He's one of God's little lambs. He's a special sheep in God's flock."

My heart was smitten with sympathy as my mind began to ponder her words. Only a few minutes before, I had counseled the family of the victim of her son's crime. Their thoughts about her son burned with intense, spiteful anger, and their words were a lot different from this mother's description of one of God's special sheep.

Staring back at this heartbroken woman, I gave thanks to God that I was no longer the same man I used to be in the early years of my criminal justice career. The old me was mean, unsympathetic, and would have told her: "Lady, you need to face reality. Your son is not a good boy and is certainly not one of God's special sheep. He is only a wolf in sheep's clothing, pulling the wool over your eyes. Your son is a cold-blooded murderer. He is a despicable, dangerous criminal who is about to get exactly what he deserves!"

Instead, the new me gently and sincerely replied: "Yes, ma'am, I know that your son is a good boy and one of God's special sheep. I am so sorry that you both have to go through this. I am so sorry." I continued to ponder her statement and thought about how my heart had been enabled to answer her as I did.

The transformation of my character was a process that took place gradually over many difficult years of learning critically important life lessons in a setting that had been the most brutally violent and emotionally ruthless classroom on earth. Breaking old, insensitive habits and changing warped thinking had been a long, daily struggle. After more than two decades in that developmental battle, I ended my prison career; but I had a lot more growing and maturing to do. I have come a long way from the confused, angry young man I used to be. As I share the stories of the journey into the depths I sank, you might come to despise the old me. You should. I do too.

☒ Shattered Safety

I grew up on the south side of Houston—a scrappy, redneck, but easygoing *Happy Days* Richie Cunningham sort of guy. Our neighborhood, like many others in the seventies, was quiet and, for the most part, peaceful. Neighbors knew their neighbors and crime took place "somewhere else—not here."

And then one night during my last year of high school, everything changed. It was all over the news:

" Bodies of 27 young boys found in shallow graves! "
Abducted—abused—murdered

Even more startling was that it took place only a few blocks from our home.

Our family was shaken; our neighborhood was horrified; the city was in disbelief; the nation was stunned. What kind of monster(s) could do such a thing? Their names: Elmer Wayne Henley, Dean Corll, and David Brooks. Doors that were never locked before were now shut tight. Parents who once allowed their children to roam free were extra protective. The secure feeling of a safe place to live was gone forever.

I was seventeen at the time. Some of those victims were about my age. I could have been one of them. The story was on everyone's lips for months. Why? Why here? I had questions too, but not a lot of answers. I do recall that one of our neighbors, known for his "religious" background, had much to say regarding what the "Word of the Lord" tells us about how to handle dangerous criminals.

I considered myself a Christian. Although I was raised Catholic, I was an uncommitted Catholic; I paid no attention to what went on at church and attended only when my parents insisted—but that had stopped early in my teen years. It had been a long time since I darkened a church doorway.

A year later, I had all but dismissed the neighbor's "Word of the Lord." But then, as a young student at Sam Houston State in Huntsville, Texas, I found myself in the middle of a class discussion of morality issues. The topic turned to the death penalty.

"Carter! What's your opinion?" the professor asked.

(Gulp.) How can I be inoffensive and as neutral as possible? Make no enemies here. It's a long time to the end of the semester. Pause . . . pause . . . pause.

"I suppose that it's all right, but personally I could never be a part of it," I hesitatingly replied. That comment only resulted in sharp opinions and objections from both sides of the debate. Rather than meet my goal of not making enemies, I succeeded in making more than anticipated. So much for fence-straddling. At the end of the session, I walked out, my head spinning in confusion and uncertainty.

Late that Friday night, as most nights, Huntsville was desolate and fog was rolling in. As I stood on my dorm balcony, looking out on the lifeless, dormant town, the slow, bellowing moan of a steam whistle inside the state penitentiary less than a mile away announced through the darkness that all was well at the prison.

As much as the local residents tried to ignore its existence, the dismal wailing of that whistle would not let the citizens rest without sounding its grim reminder that Huntsville's "bastille" was still there—lurking and real. Subconsciously, everyone in town would listen for silence after the first long whistle blast—one blast said "all is well"; three blasts meant trouble, danger, or an inmate had escaped.

Through the thick fog, I could barely see the outline of the dark, foreboding 150-year-old fortress, completely surrounded by a huge brick wall that guardedly obscured anything inside and was true to its name: the Walls. Deep inside was the extension of death row—the execution chamber. I could not imagine how anyone could possibly work there. Only two months earlier, several members of the prison staff were taken hostage, and two were killed by inmates. There could not be a worse place of employment on earth.

I would never have anticipated that less than a year later, in desperation to meet college expenses, I, Tim Carter, would become a prison guard—but, I assumed, only temporarily, until I finished college. And, as unthinkable as it was at the time, I would eventually make a career in an institution of violence and mayhem, culminating as a member of the "death squad," the exclusive group responsible for the execution of the condemned. By the time my penal career ended, I had personally assisted in the legal deaths of over 150 human beings.

☒ The Walls

The world of the penitentiary is filled with pits of pain and darkness. As a new recruit, I would step into each and every one of them. What a bizarre and amazing path my life was about to take. I saw nothing but complete darkness in the beginning of the journey.

I vividly recall my first trip to the Walls. I swallowed hard as the first crash gate slammed securely behind me. I was locked inside! When the second gate slammed shut, my knees grew weak. Suspended high overhead, in a large cage out of anyone's reach, was a guard who controlled all of the crash gates that allowed entrance into or exit out of the prison. If the guards needed to stay in cages for protection, I was in trouble!

As one crash gate after another slammed shut behind my back, the sinister atmosphere of the institution tore away what courage I may have thought I had. Realizing my complete loss of control and freedom, I felt like a lamb being led to the slaughter.

The deeper I walked into the unit, the stronger the indescribable odor of the musty old structure and its grim world. I stayed so close to the sergeant leading me that had he stopped abruptly, I would have bumped awkwardly into his heels. He displayed no fear of the hundreds of inmates standing in the crowded recreation yard through which he led me, but a cold chill came over me. Every inmate was staring directly at me—none smiling—just checking me out. I passed within inches of many of them. Some smirked and made degrading and suggestive remarks. These scar-faced convicts were big and mean. I had always considered myself to be a self-confident, high-energy guy and thought I was reasonably tough—but not nearly this tough. I couldn't believe they were all allowed to be out in the open like that and not locked up.

I thought to myself, "If I can get out of here alive, I'll never come back!"

Yet for whatever reason, I did go back the next day, and the next, and the next. For the first several months, it was a daily decision to continue the job or quit. But I survived the training and was first assigned to the Wynne Unit on the north side of Huntsville. A gruesome scene awaited as I entered the gate on my first day. An inmate lay dead on the ground, his body charred and smoking. He had fallen onto a live transformer and had been electrocuted. The word went out, but was never proven, that his working partner responsible for holding the ladder had purposefully made him fall. What a first impression!

Orientation included assignments to most of the various tasks performed by all the regular guards. My first duty was the guard tower, one of the only places where guns are allowed and, in fact, required. Having spent hours in the East Texas woods, I was no stranger to firearms. But the thought of looking down the barrel of a high-powered rifle aimed at a living human being was far different from setting the crosshairs on a ten-point buck. In training we had to promise that, no matter what, we would shoot to kill—never thinking of our target as a human, but as a dangerous wolf who himself would kill if he were not stopped. Fortunately, I never had to keep that promise.

☒ Kindness Is Weakness

In cellblock duty, my mentor was an experienced officer named Wayne. He was twice my age, tough as nails, and afraid of nothing. His was the ubiquitous movie image of a prison guard. Although he was only about forty years old, his skin was hard and leathery, his hands were heavily calloused, his voice was deep and coarse, and his gray hair belied his age.

He didn't say much at first. When we did bed check, he would just hand me a pencil and tablet and motion for me to follow. Separated from each other, we walked the sixteen "runs" (each run containing twenty-six cells) and took inventory of our "stock." If our individual counts didn't match, we did it all again, then compared our count to the captain's log, which all had better agree, or else. . . .

Wayne's constant piece of advice for me was to forget everything I was told in the training academy. It became very clear that he considered the academic side of training to be garbage—very different from his practical view of guard duty. In the middle of the graveyard shift, after midnight when all was quiet and the lights were dim, we'd have time for my personal schooling. He'd pull a chair up right in front of mine—face-to-face. He'd speak slowly and deliberately. One of the first things he said was, "You seem to be a nice guy, but that can be a problem. . . . You see, in here, nice guys don't finish last—they just don't finish. . . . Know what I mean?"

Sometimes he would just sit and stare at me until he was sure that he had my undivided attention. One nugget of Wayne's wisdom still echoes in my mind: "Son, I like you, and I want to see you survive. But in prison, kindness is weakness, and if you're one of those 'religious nuts' you'll get eaten alive." I assured him that he had nothing to worry about, especially the religious part. At that point in my life, the only thing I had faith in was myself and the fellow officers I knew I could trust. I hadn't been to Catholic Mass in a long time, and my only opinion of church was that it was mostly a meaningless ritual. I was a self-centered kid, consumed with sports and a girlfriend.

Wayne stressed how manipulative and dangerous inmates could be. It was critical that we stick together. He made it clear that inside these walls, I would have to prove my manliness. I hung on his every word, daring myself to not show any sign of weakness—which meant having to walk (and sometimes cross) a critical ethical line, a line I willingly violated without blinking an eye.

It did not take long for me to learn personally that all the dangers Wayne warned me of were very real. When prisoners were not manipulating and scheming against the officers, they were preying upon, assaulting, and raping each other. I learned how to out-hate, out-cuss, and out-con the hardest of convicts or guards. Recruits who appeared weak, gentle, or compassionate had short careers in the penal system. I vowed that I would fit in and become a valuable asset to the team. I wanted to become as tough as Wayne.

Looking at me now, in my fifties and several times a grandfather, few would believe that I could once bench press twice my weight. I was quick, agile, muscular, and had little difficulty standing my ground and proving I was one not to be reckoned with. I enjoyed fighting prisoners. Compassion and lenience were left behind, replaced by a keen attentiveness to winning the war against inmates. Mentally and emotionally I became as hard as a rock, and my heart became equally calloused and insensitive.

The penitentiary was a classroom that made an impressionable student out of me. Like a stern schoolmaster, it demanded my full attention as its student. Like a hot branding iron, it was determined to leave permanent reminders of every lesson it taught. Within the first year at the prison, all of my naïveté and innocence was completely annihilated. The discomforts I used to feel in the Sam Houston State University classrooms were like preschool playtime compared to the prison. This prison curriculum was shaping every aspect and direction in my life, but it was about to be interrupted by an unexpected detour.

CHAPTER 2

Shaped by a Turbulent Transition

Not long after I married my girlfriend, her father (who lived one hundred miles away) became seriously ill. I left college, my prison career, and Huntsville to move down to Liberty, Texas, and help the family make it through the crisis. The prison career was over and left behind . . . or so I thought.

While helping my in-laws in Liberty, I took a job as a steel worker at a mill that made oil-field drilling pipes. Unlike most positions in the prison environment, while at the steel-pipe mill, I remained at one isolated workstation all day — every day. I found myself stationed near a co-worker named Bobby Curry. Bobby's character was the exact opposite of all of my prison buddies. He was a responsible, hard worker, but he was a very kindhearted and gentle-natured guy. I initially did not trust Bobby for those very reasons, but when I realized that I was no longer in a war against criminals, I lightened up and came to heavily respect his character. Bobby was a Christian, but he was not like any religious person I had ever known. He was patient with my foul language and rough prison-guard attitude. He knew I was not religious, but he was never judgmental, condemning, or critical, and he never pushed his religion on me. All of that caused me to trust him completely. Over a long period of time, Bobby's subtle Christian influence aroused my curiosity.

I recall telling him that I supposed I believed in Jesus, but I didn't believe in any of those fairy tales in the Bible like Adam and Eve, Noah's ark, or Jonah and the whale. He told me that Jesus spoke about all of those things. He explained that if we believe in Jesus, we have to believe in those things too. I never realized that. His answers to some of my questions caused me to pick up and read from a Bible for the first time in my life. The more I read from the Bible, the more fascinating truths I learned about God that I never recalled hearing in all my childhood years of attending Catholic Mass.

I had been mostly disconnected from church for years but was so excited about my newfound interest in the Bible that I went to the Catholic church in Liberty, Texas, to ask their priest about many of the questions I had. I was shocked and deflated to be received by the priest with a rebuke rather than with joy. He sharply criticized my efforts to read the Bible and explained that only in the presence and under the direction of a priest could anyone ever truly understand what needs to be taken from Scripture. He told me that everything I needed to know was in the weekly readings of Catholic Mass and that reading the Bible on my own was a recipe for confusion and trouble. I left there totally confused and even disheartened that I had to either read the Bible against the priest's stern warning or return to the boring rituals of the Catholic Mass that I despised so much. I decided to do both. I started reading the Bible aggressively and asked Bobby Curry all of my questions, but I also started attending the Catholic Mass once again because that was the only church I had ever known.

A short while later, the steel mill shut down, Bobby and I went separate ways, and I lost his influence in my life. My father-in-law's health situation also became manageable enough to allow me to return to Huntsville to work for the prison again and go back to college.

☒ An Agent of God's Wrath

When I went back to work for the prison, I was stationed at the Goree Unit on the south side of Huntsville. Originally a female prison unit, it had been recently converted into a unit for male inmates. As a newly established men's facility, all of the other prison units took advantage of the opportunity to get rid of their worst troublemakers by reclassifying them and shipping them all to Goree. My warden said that the other units flushed their commodes and we got all of their junk. That meant that we had quite a collection of misfits, which made it a turbulent and violent place.

Not only was our inmate population filled with some of the worst undesirables, but things in the Texas prison system had also changed in the few years I was gone. A new federal court order had decreed numerous reform laws that heavily changed the way prisons were allowed to treat inmates. I learned that inmates now had many rights that they certainly did not have when I was working there before. The most shocking news I learned was that under these new laws, some of my co-workers at the Wynne Unit—co-workers I admired and respected –had been found guilty of inmate abuse and sentenced to prison. A cold chill ran up and down my spine when I realized that if I had not been unexpectedly yanked out of my Wynne Unit career when I had been, I would most likely have landed in the same predicament as my friends and been sentenced to prison myself. I realized that God removed me from a bad influence just in the nick of time and stationed me next to Bobby Curry in a whirlwind of transitions that was working together for my good.

Once at the Goree Unit, however, I quickly adapted to the new way of fighting inmates within the guidelines of the federally imposed major-use-of-force policies and began fighting inmates far more often and far more violently than ever before. The federal decree had caused a power vacuum that, along with the creation of prison gangs in Texas, caused the severe, bloody violence inside the penitentiary to increase drastically. The "war" against inmates was far more serious and deadly than it had ever been.

A bizarre twist in my personal situation was that I was back at the prison, but was in the precarious situation and risk of becoming the very religious person I hated and knew could not survive in that environment. I was now hooked on reading the Bible and back to attending Catholic Mass. I knew that kindness was weakness and that religious guards were not trusted, so I was in a quandary of how to be effective in the prison while trying to be a Christian. Without having Bobby Curry to ask about Bible-related questions, I became heavily influenced by a radio preacher to whom I listened constantly. This preacher had an extreme intolerance for sin, sinners, and worldly behavior. This helped me feel justified in my constant fighting with inmates, because he was a big proponent of judgment for sin and adamant that sinners needed to reap what they had sown. I resolved my quandary of how to be an effective prison guard while also being a Christian by following this radio preacher's influence, which steered me to become severely self-righteous, condemning, and judgmental. I considered myself a biblically justified and divinely anointed agent of God's wrath to impose judgment and punishment upon the sinful, despicable inmates. My new attempt at becoming a Christian was tempered with an impassioned hatred of evil people, and this fueled my zeal to aggressively fight the war against inmates.

My self-righteous version of faith and my quick and blasting condemnation of sinners soon caused me a lot of trouble. I fell back into the bad habit of being proud of my constant fighting of inmates and even brought some of the video recordings of these fights home to show my young children. I can remember my little daughter jumping up and down on the couch and cheering while watching these videos of her dad "taking care of business" inside the prison.

☒ Chow Hall Danger

Shortly after being assigned to the Goree Unit, I began serving as a chow hall officer, working in the kitchen and dining area every day. This was one of the few areas where inmates could congregate together; therefore, it was also the location of the most fights. On one occasion, I was supervising the preparation of the afternoon meal when I spotted a newly assigned inmate worker whom I perceived to be the most likely to cause insurrection for that day. The scars on his face and the prison-gang tattoos (lightning bolts) on both sides of his neck told me as much of his story as his rap sheet. This guy's current sentence had him doing time for murder, but that was only one of several violent crimes he'd been found guilty of over the last twenty years. To make matters a little more interesting, he was a psych patient who had recently been reclassified and upgraded to moderate-care supervision, which qualified him to work for me in the kitchen.

As I issued the food preparation tools to each inmate kitchen worker, this inmate snarled at me and showed all of the body language I needed to understand that he was not at all excited about working for me that day. We sternly stared at each other for a moment in a typical officer/inmate challenging taunt. Then I handed him a razor-sharp twelve-inch butcher knife, checked his name off of the roster, and ordered him to help the other inmates cut up the slabs of meat for the beef tips we were making for dinner that afternoon. After cursing me under his breath, he slowly and reluctantly turned and did as he was told.

I issued knifes like this every day, but it still felt completely ridiculous to be arming the inmates with whom I would inevitably have several confrontations throughout the day. I should mention that I had no weapon of my own. As soon as I checked out all of the knives, I walked around the sixty-gallon stirring pots and out to the serving-line area just in time to see two inmate line workers "go off" on each other. (That's what we called it when inmates began to fight). Thankfully, these two inmates had not been issued any knives and were only pummeling each other's faces with their fists. As I ran toward the fighters in a full sprint, I saw one of them grab a four-foot metal stirring paddle and swing it at the other inmate's head.

Just as his weapon was about to crush the other inmate's scull, I slammed into him with a flying tackle and drove him against the wall. The force of the impact of my shoulder against his torso dislodged the weapon from his hands and thwarted his attempt to hit a home run with the other inmate's head. I kept the inmate pressed firmly against the wall, twisted his arms behind his back, and began to apply handcuffs. While I was restraining him, however, I turned to observe the other fighter. Just as I feared, he was fast approaching to take advantage of the vulnerable condition of the guy I was restraining. I already had my hands full and could see no way to prevent the inevitable counterassault.

Thanks be to God, one of my fellow officers tackled the other inmate just in time. A couple of minutes later, several building security officers showed up to help us. Both fighters were immobilized and escorted to lockup while we went back to preparing the meal. This was pretty much a typical day in the chow hall; we had at least one serious fight every single day. Unfortunately, I looked forward to every fight and thoroughly enjoyed every "opportunity" for meeting the sword with the sword as an agent of God's wrath.

***

I was promoted to lieutenant at the Goree Unit. In this position I still fought a lot, but my main responsibility in fights was to make sure that they were carried out with the new federal reform guidelines to prevent brutality. I recall one incident when one of my sergeants called me on the radio to report a disturbance in our maximum security cellblock. When I arrived at the scene, I could see that an inmate was out in the hallway in front of the cellblock, refusing to comply with orders to return to his cell. The inmate was being escorted without restraints from the shower to his cell when he broke away from the escorting officers and became violent. The defiant inmate was threatening to kill any guard that came close or tried to subdue him. He also demonstrated his rage by destroying a table in the dayroom hallway. I ordered our response team to suit up in riot gear while I tried to reason with the inmate.

Approximately fifty inmates were locked up inside their cells on that particular cellblock, which had a full view of the incident, and the threatening inmate was doing his best to put on a big show for his audience. I quickly realized that all of the inmates watching from inside their cells were encouraging the insurrectionist to go ahead and kill me. It felt like the threatening inmate and I were two gladiators in an arena filled with spectators cheering for blood.

In compliance with the use-of-force policy, the entire incident was being videotaped, so I was careful to do everything according to legal guidelines. When the inmate cursed me, I calmly responded with an official warning. When he threatened me more severely, I answered with a final request for compliance. At that point, the inmate became extremely agitated that I was showing no signs of fear or alarm over his tirade, so he decided to try to make good on his threat in front of the other inmates. I was standing only about ten feet away from him when he picked up a fairly large piece of metal and threw it as hard as he could right at my face.

Despite the fact that I was a hard-nosed, judgmental, poor witness for the Lord, God was good to me. He protected my life, my health, my dignity, and my authority all in one split second. In a David versus Goliath type of miraculous intervention, God caused me to remain cool, calm, and collected. Without flinching or ducking out of the way, I was able to catch the torpedoing projectile with one hand just before it reached my nose. Without taking my eyes off of the assaultive inmate, I gently tossed the piece of metal on the ground beside me. This brought a loud roar of oohs and aahs from the gallery of inmate spectators. One of them commented that he had seen a catch just like that when Brooks Robinson snagged a line drive off the bat of Mickey Mantle.

Out of the corner of my eye, I could see that the response team had just arrived and was assembling behind me to await my orders. I told the inmate that I was giving him his final warning to turn around and allow me to place restraints on him. I waited a few seconds for his response. When his verbal abuse and increased threats made it clear that he was only entrenched in further defiance, I gave a slight nod to the team.

Like racehorses bounding out of the chutes when the gates are opened, the team rushed past me, tackled the inmate, and bent his body into the best position for me to apply handcuffs and leg irons. The gallery of inmate spectators suddenly became very quiet as the subdued inmate groaned and yelled in pain at the treatment he was receiving. The video cameras were still recording all of this, so after I saw that the inmate was sufficiently immobilized, I ordered my officers to ease up and not hurt him any more than was necessary. The assailant and the onlooking inmates got the clear message that there was zero tolerance for any inmate who would threaten and assault officers. I wanted to impose maximum painful consequences to achieve deterrence. My actions were legal and I was a legitimate asset to the departmental mission to keep peace and control crime, but it was my self-righteous attitude that was skewed. I felt that I was doing the best possible thing by zealously punishing evil people as often and as brutally as I legally could under the color of state law and the authority of God's Law.

☒ What Have I Become?

This legalistic version of my thoughts about faith began to take its toll, however, as my commitment to an attitude of judgmental condemnation eventually caught up with me. My attitude carried over into my personal life. My wife became understandably unappreciative of my holier-than-thou countenance and overall condescending disposition. Even if I never told her directly that I thought she was going to hell for not being holy enough, I sure made her feel that way. My form of religion was very "finger-pointing" critical. I made her feel like God didn't approve of her and that I didn't either. She often mentioned that I made her feel as though any attempt of hers to disagree, argue, or fight against me was to fight against God. This drove a big wedge between us that I stubbornly ignored, holding fast to my convictions. I lost that marriage, and I deserved the painful consequences. I was so aloof that it was many months after the divorce before I fully realized how many people I had hurt, how wrong I had been, and what all I had done.

My self-confidence suffered an additional blow during that same season of life when I sustained a severe shoulder injury while competing in power weight lifting. That injury ended my ability to ever lift weights again. I had been trusting in my personal physical strength rather than in the Lord, and suddenly my ability to maintain that strength was gone.

If these two life defeats weren't enough in that same season of life, I also totaled my car in a high-speed accident that came close to killing me. This downward spiral of one crushing blow after another came to a head one day as I was walking through the prison cellblocks. I was a captain at the time and was conducting a security check of the solitary confinement cellblock when I received the unpleasant combination of both a verbal and physical assault. As I walked past the cell of an angry inmate, he cursed and severely insulted me, threw a cup full of urine all over me, then spit in my face. He was locked inside his cell with steel bars between us, so the assault was limited to the dousing I had just received. But the assault itself didn't bother me. This sort of thing happened to segregation tank officers every day back then. What happened about thirty seconds later is what made a lasting impression on me.

I stepped into a restroom to wipe off the mess, and while standing in front of the mirror, staring at the spit on my face and my urine-soaked uniform, a strange and dark feeling swept over me. Right there, alone in that tiny, dim-lit, musty room, my mind drifted off into a sinking feeling of gloomy defeat like nothing I had ever before experienced. I felt like that image in the mirror of a urine-soaked face full of spit was a very appropriate and accurate reflection of exactly who I was. I stared at my reflection and in the silence of my mind asked myself, "What have I become?" How in the world did I ever get this messed up? All of the recent personal failures and disappointments I had incurred came crashing down on me in that moment. It was a dose of sobering self-evaluation that was long overdue. The assessment was loss of family, credibility, purpose, direction, motivation, and even faith. I finally realized that I had drifted miles away from the God I thought I was serving. I was broken and alone. I stared at the image of a failure, exhaled my last breath of hope, and gave up. I made up my mind to throw in the towel, to quit that prison career, and to relocate to a place far enough away where no one would know what a failure I had become.

CHAPTER 3

Shaped by the Serpent/Dove Principle

X Wise as Serpents; Innocent as Doves

The next day, I made a quick visit to Sam Houston State University in an attempt to speak to a criminology professor, Dr. George Beto. He had once been the director of the entire Department of Criminal Justice in Texas, and I had heard that he was a strong Christian. He was an extremely busy man and my time with him was very brief. I only wanted to ask him two questions. He allowed and answered the first question. I never got around to asking the second. I first asked him how it was possible for him to be an effective prison employee and be a Christian at the same time. I was going to ask next if he thought I should resign or if it would help anything for me to transfer to a small, remote Texas prison unit over six hundred miles away to get away from my failures and get my head together.

I told Dr. Beto that I had been reading the Bible for several years and that I believed my calling in life was to serve the Lord by fighting the good fight—which, in my opinion, was the war against evil criminals—by being an agent of God's wrath and judgment upon them. I told him I knew very well that in prison, kindness is weakness and that meek Christians don't last long. I gave Him a brief description of my efforts and failures and asked how in the world he ever succeeded in prison management as a Christian. He respectfully, yet firmly answered by reciting one Scripture verse. It was Matthew 10:16: "I am sending you out as sheep in the midst of wolves, so be wise [or shrewd] as serpents and innocent [or gentle] as doves." He then explained that I had it half right. He said that I was very good at being as wise as a serpent, but I appeared to be a complete failure at being as innocent (or gentle) as a dove. He then stated that it is necessary for all Christians to be both of those in order to represent Christ properly. He told me that I was like most people in that I desired to follow Jesus on my own terms by picking and choosing which Scripture passages support my personal views while intentionally ignoring other passages that are critical and against my personal perspective.

He explained that inside the state penitentiary we must be both wise as a serpent and also innocent as a dove, but this is impossible without the help of the Holy Spirit. Being as innocent as a dove requires dying to self and walking humbly before the Lord as a repentant sinner. He told me that though it seemed I had been failing at that, the Gospel promises that the Lord wants to forgive my pride and enable me to die to self. He shared that working on the balance between these two for the rest of my life is all I need to know. Then he told me to go back to work and let the grace of the Gospel speak to me, not just the Law of God. And that was it. He was out of the time that he was able to give me.

I left his office feeling tremendously better, but not quite knowing why. I wanted to know more about this way of thinking about reading and applying the Bible, so I found out where he went to church and I started attending there. However, I never received any further counsel from Dr. Beto because he moved to Austin soon after that, then died a short time later. Although Dr. Beto was no longer at his church, I quickly discovered that God was there in a bigger way than I had ever know Him before. The nature of teaching at the church ran in heavy contrast to the radio preacher to whom I was so devoted, as it stressed much more mercy and grace. The services also offered a different and seemingly more meaningful method and expression of God's forgiveness than the Catholic Masses I had been attending.

X Starting Over in Christ

I eventually stopped listening to the radio preacher and stopped attending the Catholic Mass. Dr. Beto's church (part of The Lutheran Church—Missouri Synod) became my church. I began to realize that he was right. I had been selectively reading and applying the Bible to fit my preferences. The embarrassing part of this stage in my development was that I was recognizing a need to apply the whole Word of God and be less judgmental, but it seemed that I was incapable of translating that into action. Not only had I failed at dying to self in the past, but I was still failing. My growing desire to squash my legalistic pride was met with a sobering and embarrassing inability: it felt like my heart was so deeply ingrained into self-righteous thinking that it was completely resistant to change. I repentantly asked my pastor for his help, and he explained to me that God has forgiven me and that He was enabling me to conform to His Word. He said, however, that I had developed my thinking and behavioral habits over many years and those habits were like an addiction. He said that God was bigger than my biggest and most long-established addictions, but real and permanent changes probably would not happen overnight; salvation happens instantly, but transformation takes time.

My first moment of truth and self-examination occurred in that little bathroom in solitary confinement, staring in the mirror at the spit and urine all over me. I desperately needed every one of those painful consequences of my failures to bring me low enough to receive a strong dose of humbleness. The most crushing abasement, however, came in realizing how seriously I was addicted to my sin. Despite my mind comprehending the truth I needed to conform to, my body could not. I continued to enjoy violent confrontations and to adhere only to the wisdom of a serpent principle. During that dark season, I read a passage in 1 Timothy 1:13–16 that described me perfectly:

Formerly I was a blasphemer, persecutor, and insolent opponent. But I received mercy because I had acted ignorantly in unbelief, and the grace of our Lord overflowed for me with the faith and love that are in Christ Jesus. The saying is trustworthy and deserving of full acceptance, that Christ Jesus came into the world to save sinners, of whom I am the foremost. But I received mercy for this reason, that in me, as the foremost, Jesus Christ might display His perfect patience as an example to those who were to believe in Him for eternal life.

I had to own that passage and admit my faults, but I found great hope in it. It's amazing to me that the apostle Paul actually wrote that message to "Timothy." Like Paul, I, Timothy, was a worse sinner than those I was condemning and judging. Like Paul, I was a perfect target for God to display His amazing character of patience, grace, and mercy to those who clearly know they don't deserve it. Like Paul, I needed to be spiritually killed in order to be made alive in Christ. My skewed ideas of serving the Lord had to be crushed in order to begin the transformation process of falling in line with His plans instead of my own. I prayed for a miracle to break free from the bondage I was in.

I found a couple of Scripture verses that I learned and repeated in prayer before the Lord over and over. James 4:10 says: "Humble yourself before the Lord, and He will exalt you." I desperately needed Him to exalt me, to lift me up, so I asked for the ability to humble myself before Him. Boy, oh boy would He ever answer that prayer! The other verse was 2 Corinthians 12:9a: "My grace is sufficient for you, for My power is made perfect in weakness." Both of these verses gave me hope in my constant failures to become as innocent, or gentle, as a dove. I found myself totally dependent upon the Lord to deliver and restore me.

Not long after that, my life and prison career underwent many abrupt changes. I found myself transferred to the Walls Unit under bizarre circumstance that I neither had control over nor desired. A captain at the Walls Unit married his supervisor's daughter, which called for him to be transferred to a different prison unit. He and I were asked to swap unit assignments. It was a sudden and unexpected change, but I quickly began to consider that this could be a blessing. I became optimistic about the possibility to start over, away from most of the former co-workers around whom I was content to remain the old me. Within a few years, I also started a new relationship and re-married. My wife, Jill, was also struggling with her transformation, which gave her the extreme patience to put up with my instability.

X   The Death Squad

Transferring to a new unit seemed to be an answer to my prayer to be delivered from my bad habits. God arranged for me to escape the atmosphere where I had grown comfortable remaining the old me. I was certainly still in prison, but working at the Walls Unit provided a new atmosphere with new relationships that might allow me to make some fresh changes. Maybe I could now be in a better position to actually follow Dr. Beto's advice of dying to self and trying to walk more humbly before the Lord.

In further answer to my prayers, God did indeed enable me to slowly but surely make changes in my heart and my actions. Month after month at the Walls Unit, I progressively felt a little bit less wise as a serpent and slightly more gentle as a dove. Although the changes were slow, I noticed God working them in me, and I was so thankful for them. I suppose God knew I would need a new heart more than ever, because the biggest life change of all was about to happen.

The Huntsville Prison Unit, more commonly known as "The Walls Unit", is the location where all death row executions take place in the state of Texas. I spent two-thirds of my prison career working (and living) at this unit.

I was working as a disciplinary hearing judge for the Texas Department of Criminal Justice's (TDCJ) internal court system at the Walls Unit. This placed me in a prime position for an appointment to the death squad, and soon after arriving there I was asked to join that team. The old me would have excitedly jumped at the opportunity, but I knew of many other supervisors who strongly desired that appointment, so I told the administration that when and if they absolutely had to have me for that team, I would join, but until then, I'd decline. That actually worked for a couple of years until the day came when I was told that I really was needed . . . and my life was then changed forever. What a stark testimony of the truth in Proverbs 16:9: "The heart of man plans his way, but the LORD establishes his steps."

As I was about to begin serving as a member of the death squad, my mind raced back to the same thoughts I had many years ago as a young college student. Back then, I had never read one word of Scripture and was clueless as to God's will concerning capital punishment. After years of reading the Bible and going through a turbulent journey of selective, misapplication of His Word, I was finally on the right track of a healthy balance of being wise as a serpent yet gentle as a dove. However, I still found myself harboring fresh uncertainties about God's will for government executions. I prayed and specifically searched God's Word for His counsel. I knew that God's Law did indeed ordain some people to be agents of His wrath and wise as a serpent, but now I also knew that Christian public servants must also be gentle as doves. The Lord gave me guidance concerning His will. That guidance, however, came through a long, tumultuous tug-of-war that kept me humbly on my knees and deep in God's Word, studying that subject for many years.

I discovered that it was irresponsible and virtually impossible to give a quick casual answer of yes or no, right or wrong, to the question of whether capital punishment was God's will or not. It took a very long journey through many years of emotional, spiritual struggle and prayer for me to learn all that the Lord revealed to me about what really matters to Him concerning mercy, justice, and government executions.

I was shown many different dimensions of human suffering surrounding the capital punishment arena that profoundly concern the heart of God. I observed that on both sides of the controversy and in every aspect of that suffering, Satan was deceitfully causing some people to interpret the cause of their pain and suffering connected to capital murder and capital punishment as their justification for completely rejecting God. Each dimension of the capital punishment process is steeped in sad, gloomy darkness, and I was shown that there is a serious need for servants of the Lord to serve Him in the middle of that darkness, pointing people to His light. With that understanding, and numerous Bible passages of specific guidance that I will share later in this book, I knew that I could serve the Lord on the death squad.

[X] The Death House

Although I had worked for the TDCJ for many years, I had not yet been exposed to any part of the execution process. I can still remember my first walk into the death house and inside the death chamber; it was an unforgettable occasion. As the warden led me down into the death house, I remember asking myself if my heart was really ready to step off into this way of life. I trusted the Lord, because at this stage of my development, I would not have chosen or planned this course for my life. As we passed through the huge steel doors to walk inside the death house, all of my senses became immediately aware that we had just stepped out of a bright warm environment outside, down into a dark, cold atmosphere inside. It was exceptionally quiet and motionless.

The death house is an old structure and appeared to have been heavily used over the years. I was shown the row of holding cells, which has the capacity to house multiple death row inmates. The death house has a shower facility to offer the inmate the opportunity to wash off and change into fresh clothing a few hours prior to execution. There is also an extra-high-security holding cell for any final visits from an attorney. This cell has a fine wire mesh allowing only sight and sound but prohibiting the passing of anything from the visitor to the inmate and vice-versa. Across from the holding cell is a red light next to a telephone that links a direct hotline from the governor's office and represents an inmate's last chance for a stay of execution or reprieve. Finally, at the end of the hallway, is the green door.

"This is it," the warden explained, as he turned the key and slowly squeaked open the thick steel door to reveal the death chamber. Peering inside, I swallowed hard as I saw it for the first time. There it was—illuminated and positioned solidly in the center of the room: the death gurney. As I stepped in, it was even colder inside the chamber. I stood there in silence, gazing at a sight that looked about as welcoming as an open coffin. It seemed to have a presence about it that silently proclaimed that it was ready . . . and waiting. The gurney was a flat steel table mounted on a single steel pedestal. On the table was a thin mattress and a small, white pillow. The entire gurney was lined with thick leather restraining belts and buckles for the complete immobilization of its unfortunate designee. We just stood there in silence, staring at it for a long time.

The death chamber was a small room, only about eight feet by twelve feet. The walls were a drab gray. To the left of the death gurney on one wall was a large two-way mirror. On the other side of the mirror was the room where the injection team performed its duty anonymously. An IV tube ran from a saline drip bag through a small hole in the wall to the arm support of the death gurney. Across from the one-way mirror, to the right of the death gurney, were two large windows. Behind these windows were two viewing rooms for witnesses. These rooms were side by side but separated from each other by a thick dividing wall. Each room had steel bars against their viewing windows

This is the death gurney inside of the death chamber as seen from the viewing room where I often held the witnessing families of the condemned.

Photo courtesy of Texas Department of Criminal Justice.

to prevent any chance of interruption or intervention by visitors. The death chamber had a boom microphone over the gurney to broadcast the inmate's last words over speakers mounted in each viewing room. Witnesses can hear what is said in the death chamber but the condemned inmate cannot hear anything from within the viewing rooms. As I checked it out and soaked it all in, I had the feeling of standing and viewing an old historic battlefield, imagining all of the amazing and horrible things that happened there.

Finally the warden turned to me and asked, "Are you okay?" "Sure," I replied. All new members of the death squad are tested to see how they will handle this assignment. Some never make it past the initial tour. The warden motioned for us to leave and we stepped out. As he closed the door to the death chamber and turned the key, it felt like he was tightly locking the cage of a ravenous lion. I couldn't see it anymore. It was safely locked away. But I knew it was still there, just waiting behind the huge green door.

Over the next several years, I would walk in and out of those doors hundreds of times. Because of all the sad and sobering things I witnessed there, I referred to it as "the valley of the shadow of death row." All the members of the first death squad I was a part of eventually moved on and left that assignment, yet for some reason, God allowed for me to remain on that duty and keep walking through that valley for more executions than anyone else at that time. I regularly reminded myself that God's ways are not our ways (Isaiah 55:8) and that in His wisdom, He has His reasons for allowing us to endure challenges and travel paths we would have never chosen for ourselves. Accordingly, I would come to realize the Lord's reason for allowing my assignment to the Texas Death Squad. He was shaping and equipping me to represent Him well and reflect Jesus well to all those who would have to walk through that awful valley. I would need to remind myself of His reasons over and over again in the middle of each amazing encounter that I was about to experience.

CHAPTER 4

Shaped by the Appointment to the Death Squad

When I began dealing with death row inmates and their families in the capital punishment process, I was introduced to a much wider array of human pain than routine prison life had already shown me. I was actually thankful that my heart was finally becoming more capable of feeling pain and empathy for others, but with every one of those encounters, a spiritual tug-of-war of justice versus mercy ensued. Through a lot of trial and error over many years, I discovered that exercising an appropriate balance of wisdom and gentleness was impossible without God's help. The Lord showed me that I always misrepresent Him when I apply either one more than the other. Primarily, He showed me that when I walked closely with Him, I would be in balance and He would use me to bless others in the death house. With that invigorating realization, I resolved to continue serving Him in my prison career indefinitely. Settling into that decision made prison life a little easier. I became more focused on seeking God's counsel in handling the new challenges each day would bring.

The decision to continue with my criminal justice career meant that I retained the secure income and benefits God had provided for me. The state of Texas offered some nice perks to help stimulate retention of seasoned employees, and I considered them a huge blessing. Some prison administrators and supervisors are provided the benefit of free housing, utilities, and maintenance; I was blessed with these luxuries for most of my career. However, there are usually a few drawbacks to anything that is free, and this was no exception. My state housing was on prison property, just outside the walls of the prison unit. Employees who live on prison property never get to experience leaving work behind at the end of the day. In exchange for living there rent-free, I was on-call 24/7. I had a direct hotline phone in my house for the prison to be able to call me any time for immediate response for any emergency need. Another drawback was having my little children grow up in a yard and neighborhood that was always full of inmate yard workers and maintenance crews.

Our housing arrangement really wasn't all that bad, however, and I cherished it as a wonderful blessing. Although I worked in a wolf pen, the Good Shepherd prepared me a table in the presence of my enemies and made me to lie down in the green pasture of great provisions. Living only one minute from work would allow me, on many execution days, to make the short walk home for a quick evening break before having to begin execution duty. The state of Texas used to conduct all executions at midnight, but many years ago the state changed the execution time to 6:00 p.m.

☒ Where Is God in All of This?

I was involved in so many executions that memories of those events tend to blend together. Some, however, are indelibly etched into my heart and mind forever. On one particular evening, I was using my pre-execution break to sit quietly on the couch with my wife, Jill. We had no television, radio, or music playing—only silence. I was relaxing, trying to clear my mind and mentally prepare myself for the atmosphere and environment that I was about to step into. When the clock told us it was time for me to go back to work, Jill and I held hands, prayed together for a moment, and gave each other a quick kiss; then I stood up to head for the door. Walking toward the back door, I paused to look at the framed photos of my children, Kent and Kimberly. I was emotionally consumed with the conscious awareness of how blessed I was to have a healthy, happy, loving family with no devastating challenges or crises in our lives.

As I stepped out of that comfortable, air-conditioned house into the sweltering heat, the instant discomfort seemed fitting for the equally drastic change of emotional climate. As I slowly began walking to the front door of the prison, I sensed that this walk was quite different. I was never excited about making this little stroll, but each step of this particular trip was becoming more difficult. It was a stifling hot day in Huntsville, and the Texas summer sun was still lingering high and harsh at five o'clock in the evening. The thick humidity was siphoning my energy to carry out an all too common task of executing still one more death row inmate. This was our third execution within a week, and our schedule for the rest of the year looked almost as busy.

At that moment, however, the grueling heat and hectic schedule were not wearing on me nearly as much as the attempt to mentally change gears from basking in the contentment, joy, and tranquility of my own peaceful family life to the inevitable pain and agony of the people I would soon be meeting. I knew full well that whether I was visiting with the condemned inmate or working with the families of the victim(s) and of the condemned, everyone involved was going to be angry, hurting, or both.

For some reason, my routinely one-minute walk to the prison had drawn out to over five minutes. My pace was slowing. I knew it wasn't a physical problem. I was not having a stroke or heart attack. But with every step I took, I realized that my pace was being hindered by the feeling of an increasingly heavier burden on my soul for all the hearts full of despair and misery that were about to be entrusted to my care. I certainly did not dread meeting or dealing with these people. I actually welcomed the possibility of serving them in some small way as an opportunity, not a sacrifice. My heart always hurt for these people, and I yearned more than ever to help them carry their burdens.

As I continued my walk, I became overwhelmed with the feeling that I was mostly powerless to actually help the witnessing families avoid or overcome the inevitable pain that was about to consume them. This powerlessness had become an emotional burden that felt like an extra hundred pounds to carry. Still fifty yards from the front door, I came to a complete stop. The weight of this inability to help those I had developed such a compassion for was dragging me down so much that I found myself standing completely still, just staring up into the sky, asking God for help and understanding. Oblivious to any potential distractions from my surroundings, my heart was reaching for guidance and direction, silently calling out to my God.

My heart was suddenly reminded of 2 Chronicles 20. In this passage, King Jehoshaphat cried out to the Lord that he was powerless against the challenges coming against him and he did not know what to do; but his eyes were on God, looking for some kind of rescue. That was exactly what I was feeling at that very moment. The Lord's answer to him was that the battle was not Jehoshaphat's, but God's. The Lord told him that if he would just take a firm stand against the enemy, he would not have to fight that fight, but the Lord would fight for him. I remembered my pastor once explained that God wanted Jehoshaphat to be humbled before Him and to become totally dependent on the Lord. I remembered that being humbled was one of my greatest needs, so I took Jehoshaphat's counsel as my own. I realized that I also was totally helpless apart from the Lord, but if I would simply stand firm against the enemy, I would not have to fight that fight on my own. All of the human trial and tragedy I encountered on death row execution nights was always bigger than my ability to handle; I couldn't fix those hurting people. But God was bigger. He would do the work of caring for those hurting hearts. All I needed to do was stand firm against the enemy and God would enable me to represent Him well.

With that gentle touch from the Holy Spirit, my burden was immediately lifted—and my body was strengthened. With renewed energy and a clear mind, I completed my walk to the prison. As I ascended the steps to the front door of the penitentiary, I actually had a skip in my step as I was still looking up to heaven, praying for God to fight the good fight for me, and trusting the Lord to do exactly that.

I walked into the prison and back to the death house where the condemned inmate was eating his last meal and talking quietly with the prison chaplain, Rev. Jim Brazzil. I joined in on this time of counsel and prayer for a while. The lie-down team was assembling while the hearse from the local funeral home was backing up to await a body that was currently very much alive and quite healthy. After spending some time with the condemned inmate, I checked my watch and saw that it was 5:30 p.m. It was time to prepare the witnesses for their trip into the unit and back toward the death house.

In my first year on the death squad, I performed several different roles in the process. After being on the squad for many years, however, I had pretty much settled into one primary role. My biggest responsibility in every execution was to spend time first with the condemned inmate, then with his family, then with the families of the victims. I would address our security concerns with each family group and assess their ability to participate before bringing them inside the prison, where I would maintain constant control of them as they witnessed the execution.

Although this was a somber task, most executions were quiet and reasonably uneventful. However, I had done this enough to know that this particular night was not going to be a "normal" night. Upon stepping into the holding room for the condemned inmate's family, my senses immediately confirmed what Chaplain Brazzil had previously warned me about. The room was full of visitors who were not in any way warm and hospitable, but rather visibly nervous and stressed. Some were pacing back and forth, and one lady was staring a hole straight through me with piercing anger and contempt. My request for them to submit to a search was received like an invitation to fight! Jim had warned me earlier that this family was not taking the execution very well, and by that point, they weren't taking me too well either. I had been in this situation many times before, but I never got used to the feeling of being so intensely hated by someone I didn't even know.

I quickly realized that the most hostile attitudes were coming from a European couple who were anti–death penalty activists. They had basically adopted this death row inmate. It is common for activists from other countries to fly to the United States to visit condemned inmates and develop strong relationships with them. These foreign anti–death penalty folks are rarely friendly to us, but the group on this particular night was aggressively unfriendly. The inmate's mother and sisters were not hostile but were definitely not in a good mood. The search I conducted on all of these people was done cautiously but thoroughly and with an extra effort to be sensitive and respectful of their emotional stress.

The rooms for questioning and searching the family of the condemned are right across the street from the entrance to the Walls Unit. We made it through the questioning and search successfully, but when I escorted them across the street, past the reporters, television cameras, and shouting protesters, the mother and one sister broke down and cried. Their emotions suddenly seemed to shift from anger to fear and brokenness. We completed our walk across the street and into the prison and eventually back to the death house. When we stepped down into the death chamber viewing area, the inmate's mother became a little weak-kneed and nauseous as she saw her son securely fastened and strapped to the gurney with an IV line hooked up to his arm. My soul grieved for her, but we had to continue. I gave the signal that we were ready, and the prison director then instructed the warden to proceed. It was clearly evident that the mother's heart was breaking to pieces, but she was trying her best to hold herself together as her daughters held her in support.

I stood behind the family and watched the mother staring at her son. She was only about ten feet away from him, but a thick glass window and steel bars stood between them. She silently leaned against the window and stroked her hand on the glass as if she were stroking her son's hair. It appeared to me as though she was remembering him as the little baby boy she had brought into the world. It seemed that she was lost in the memory of another time when she was holding and coddling her sweet, innocent little child. As tears streamed down her cheeks, I stepped forward and handed her some tissues, then stepped back and gave them all some space. The folks from Europe were standing stiff and stern, holding firmly to their anger, but I could tell that the moment was wearing hard on them too. The condemned inmate gave a calm, short last statement and bid his family and friends farewell. The young man then looked at his mother and said: "Good-bye, Mama. Don't cry, Mama." Then the warden gave the signal to the injection team.

I always pray fervently for the comfort and healing of these families at this moment, but that night I was praying with a passion! I knew the next ten seconds would set the tone for the rest of the evening, and just as I feared, when the lethal injection collapsed the inmate's lungs and he coughed his last breath, everything disintegrated. The inmate's mother was there witnessing this execution for one reason: so that her son would not have to go through this alone. For his sake she stayed strong throughout the entire proceedings and held herself together . . . until her son was dead.

Then, when he was obviously gone from this life, the dam broke. The volcano of suppressed emotions erupted. Whatever strength she had accumulated to stand up strong and straight on her own two legs instantly vanished. Suddenly she let out a blood-curdling scream of pain and agony that would break even the coldest and hardest of hearts. Her knees buckled and she crumbled to the floor where she rolled and writhed in uncontrollable and inconsolable emotional pain that I imagined would have no equal. She was crying out in a low, gut-wrenching moan: "My baby, my baby, oh dear God, my baby!"

I attempted to be of assistance, but her daughters were consoling her and I had the distinct feeling that she needed to be left alone to her only means of dealing with that kind of pain. In the midst of this troubling ordeal, I recall the voice of the enemy shouting in my ear: "Where is God in all of this?" My emotions were tugging on my heart and asking me—is it really possible for all things to work together for good for those who love Him? Even this?

Then I remembered God's counsel: if I depended totally upon Him, He would fight for me. I remembered that God promised He would never leave us nor forsake us. It was strength enough for me to know that God was right there with that mother and with me. The voice of the enemy was drowned out by my recalling the voice of my pastor teaching that any form of death was never God's desire for His sheep and that all forms of heartbreak and grieving were against God's original design. But even though He allowed the rebellion of mankind and the far-reaching consequences, He also provides His presence, comfort, and guidance.

I remembered Jesus' words: "Blessed are those who mourn, for they shall be comforted" (Matthew 5:4). The Lord enabled me to recall Psalm 91, which tells us that the Lord answers those who call upon His name and is with them in their times of trouble. The Lord used this experience and these passages of Scripture to teach me that even when His sheep are in the midst of a season of sorrowful griev- ing, we can actually be heavily blessed. When our sympathy for the afflictions of others or the regrets of our own penitent heart reduces us to mourning, we are actually showing honor to God. When we reach a moment of helplessness and collapse into God's arms with our mourning, it is indeed a blessing to know that we are being held securely in the palm of His hand. Jesus sheds light and encourage- ment on our current suffering and on our future by promising that we will be comforted. I knew that the only hope of comfort for these people was in the divine assurance that, because they were calling out to God, they most certainly were and would be blessed.

When this mother stood watching her own child die right in front of her, it gave me some insight into the depth of our heavenly Father's relatability to our suffering because He watched His own Son suffer (John 3:16). The state of Texas expected me to be in complete control of these families and this procedure, but at that moment the struggle was to keep control of myself. It wasn't easy, but I successfully fought back my own tears and any outward show of emotion even though my heart was breaking for the grieving mother. I was professional and self-controlled on the outside, but on the inside I felt her intense pain. The sound of sorrow melted my heart. The sight of despair tested my resolve. Even the European couple seemed to forget about their anger, and their countenance was transformed to compassion and respect.

There is absolutely nothing that can be said or done to truly help at a time like that, so I prayed silently and didn't speak a word to them. I remembered the Lord's counsel to be gentle as a dove and to be totally dependent upon Him, and it was indescribably comforting for me when I was. Finally, when the inmate's mother was able to gain enough composure, she allowed us to put her in a wheelchair, and we wheeled her out of the death house because she was unable to walk under her own power. The walk out of the unit was extra slow and silent except for the mother's low, muffled groaning as we went. Once out of the unit, I handed the group over to the state police officers to escort them back into the holding room.

As the procession of family and friends filed past me, one of the sisters turned to me and thanked me for "being kind and considerate." I was thankful that she felt that way, but I was surprised and puzzled by her comment, since I hadn't said or done anything but guard and escort them. As they continued to file past me, even the European man paused to thank me for caring. As they all disappeared through the doorway, I returned to the unit, reflecting on the fact that only God could transform this atmosphere from confrontational and hostile to loving and peaceful. Even though my only contribution to helping these people was fervent and passionate prayer, God does at times answer prayer dramatically . . . at times, instantly.

For the longest time, I could not understand how God would somehow comfort people through me enough to cause them to thank me, when I felt as though I had done nothing meaningful for them. But then I heard my pastor preach a sermon one Sunday that helped me understand what had happened. In many painful and heartbreaking moments for people, he said, there is nothing anyone can say or do to console or comfort them. "In these moments, we have to rely on a different source of love: God's love." The healing touches that people need cannot originate in us but can only come through us when we allow ourselves to be a vessel of God's healing love. God's love goes beyond our own ability or capacity. Therefore, we must let God extend His love through us.

Finding myself in numerous similar experiences confirmed for me why I was placed in the prison environment. I worked in the ugliest pit imaginable, yet God consistently used me to subtly but surely touch lives during those delicate and sensitive moments for the people He loves.

☒ "I See You're a Christian"

During my years in the death house, I desired to be an instrument of blessing to all the people I watched and escorted. This was especially awkward, however, when I found myself being lambasted and reviled by friends and family of condemned inmates and by anti–death penalty activists. How in the world could I ever be any kind of "blessing" to these people? Quite often, the very people I wanted to help were glaring at me and telling me that I was a murderer and that I was going straight to hell for executing people. But God helped me understand that these really are good people—people who are simply hurting and struggling with a lot of displaced anger while they are weighed down by this burden. Therefore, I was never offended or hurt by any of their actions. I believed that God intentionally allowed those regular occurrences of verbal abuse to humble me and make sure I never got comfortable with my job. Rather than having a negative reaction to people who criticized and insulted me, God allowed me to have a heart that had compassion on them, so I always prayed for and loved them.

One of the worst examples of being hated by witnesses occurred during a night when I was escorting the father and four brothers of a condemned inmate. They were so confrontational and angry that I came very close to not allowing them to come into the prison to witness the execution. This moment required a serious balance of a serpent's wisdom (or shrewdness) and a dove's innocence (or gentleness). After a polite but stern warning, and after recruiting the escort assistance of a Texas Ranger and two very large security supervisors, I allowed them in.

These witnesses were the most emotionally explosive I have ever seen. They contained their comments and actions the best they could, but their feeling of helplessness, seeing their family member die in a moment when they surely would have given their lives for him, was almost more than they could stand. The depth of love and concern for him was deeply constrained as they had to just stand there and watch. While their deep concern for their loved one was actually very admirable, at that moment, it was also very dangerous. As I stood beside them watching the inmate die, I silently prayed for their comfort and healing. Yet at the same time, my adrenaline was peaked in mental and physical preparation to "take them down" (subdue and restrain them), if necessary.

When the inmate breathed his last, the family could not contain themselves any longer and began to increasingly curse and threaten us. My warnings to calm down were completely ignored, so I opened the back door of the witness room and informed them that they would all have to leave immediately. They slowly and begrudgingly complied as we ushered them out under heavy escort. The entire escort team was cautious and vigilant but also self-controlled and patiently empathetic. I was praying that we would not have to restrain or arrest them for their conduct, but it was definitely touch and go every step of the way.

I tried to move the procession toward the prison exit as fast as I could, but in this atmosphere of controlled mayhem and tension, it felt like glaciers would move faster. When we finally made it all the way to the front gate of the prison, they began to file past me and out into the street. As they did, each one gave me the clear understanding through words and actions that they would very much like to tear me to pieces. Just when I thought the ordeal was about to come to a safe conclusion, the last guy to reach the front gate stopped, turned around, and faced me. I pushed my serpent's shrewdness to full ready position and prepared myself for the worst as he stood there, just staring at me.

Then everything changed. This man suddenly appeared to have a newfound self-awareness, as if turning on a light switch. He took a deep breath and, with a fresh attitude of self-control and peace, pointed at and touched the wristband I was wearing, saying, "I see you're a Christian." He had noticed the Scripture verse imprinted on the leather wristband I was wearing, as if that somehow did for him what it did for me every time I looked at it. It reminded me of all I heard and felt when my pastor urged us to become better witnesses and brothers in Christ. He then gave me an affirming nod and walked away.

He seemed to be convicted of his actions in the middle of a crazy and chaotic moment. It was like we were transformed from enemies to brothers. I was extremely thankful for the break in the tension, but mostly I was astonished by yet another reminder from God that He is in control and always with us, especially in the worst of times. Our Good Shepherd is always beside us with His rod and His staff to comfort us. He hears and answers our prayers and will always make a way to provide strength for the journey just when we need it the most!

☒ Behind the Scenes

The outside world has no idea what actually takes place in the microcosm of the death house. On an execution day, all of the focus of the prison staff, the media, and the public is exactly where it should be — on the condemned inmate. If, however, someone could look behind the scenes of the profile of the condemned and his crime, the extra emphasis by the prison staff for maximum security and the high-energy efforts of the media to give the best possible coverage, he or she would discover a world of its own existing at an unseen and least-considered level.

In this world, normal, average, healthy people are brought together by a very abnormal and unhealthy event. They are thrust onto a stage together to interact in roles none of them auditioned for or desired in any way. One person has to live the role of a mommy witnessing the execution of the person who suddenly took her little child out of her life by a cruel and senseless murder. Another is present as a mommy, too, but in a very different role. She has watched her son follow a path and a lifestyle that had always broken her heart, though nothing can compare to the execution day when she watches this for a final and most painful time.

A few are present because their dreams of a career in media or journalism took an unexpected turn, and suddenly they found themselves not just covering a story but witnessing a side of life that their most creative skills and abilities will never be able to adequately report and explain. Many are here to serve the public in a task for which no wage, salary, or career promotion could ever possibly compensate; only out of a sense of duty and loyalty to the people they serve can they fill their roles.

All these actors must not only fill their roles but also somehow interact together with all the others on stage without any rehearsal. Fortunately, most of the actors will visit this stage and perform this scene but once. However, when the scene is acted out and done, they will relive and replay it in their minds and in their hearts over and over again for the rest of their lives.

As for my co-workers and me, we lived on this stage. Many of us performed this scene well over a hundred times but with new and different co-actors and scripts each time. As ugly and sad as our world on this stage is, it actually has its blessed moments. There are many ways that God has stepped into this little world behind the execution scene, worked all things together for good, and turned it into a form of positive growth, blessing, and even a miracle for a lot of people.

The death house is indeed a cold and ugly place, yet the presence of the almighty God is always manifested during the execution process. There are unsuspecting recipients of the benefits of His presence, and I have never seen anyone go through the process without being touched by Him. All participants, no matter what role they are playing, come away from an execution with an undeniably larger consciousness and awareness of their own mortality. The most in-control attitudes on the faces of the most confident and self-assured people diminish while they are here. I am convinced that all participants, Christian or non-Christian, walk away needing and craving a deeper understanding of something they can't describe. They seem to know there is an undeniable and seemingly unquenchable void that only God can fill. The enemy uses this process to sow a tremendous amount of grief, despair, and confusion, but for those who look to the Good Shepherd, their void is filled with His comforting presence and their darkest hour is illuminated with hope.

What are the surviving sheep supposed to do when wolves ravage God's sheep pen? We are supposed to be wise as serpents but gentle as doves. We are to put on the whole armor of God and listen for the Shepherd's invitation to join Him in comforting those who are stricken with adversity. There are countless numbers of people all over the world suffering and hurting in many different ways who need Christian brothers and sisters to reach out to them in mercy. However, it always seemed to me that the great multitudes of people in physical and spiritual anguish are so overwhelming that all the Mother Theresas and missionaries in the world could never make any more of a difference than a drop in a bucket.

In the penitentiary it appears equally futile. For every one inmate who is saved and transformed by the Gospel, there is always a whole busload of new inmates coming in the back gate. It is an encouragement and blessing to realize that even one of these "drop in the bucket" lives is priceless to Jesus and worth all of our prayers and efforts to reach them. Whether in third world countries or local prisons, challenges are not overwhelming problems but rather tremendous opportunities to be a blessing to others and to be blessed ourselves (Matthew 25:34–36).

This is the back gate of the Walls Unit where we receive incoming new inmates and where the local funeral hearse passes through to remove executed inmates.

Here in this obscure little corner of East Texas called the death house, our own particularly awkward and ugly form of human adversity seemed insurmountable. When thrust into the middle of so many hurting and damaged people, I felt the opportunity—but I also felt powerless and inadequate for my calling. So many times, however, in simple but fervent prayer for the suffering people standing beside me, I physically saw them receive comfort and peace as I prayed for them.

God used my job to teach me that my best efforts to perform any works or deeds for His people are nothing compared to the power He displays when my weaknesses and helplessness reduce my abilities alone to prayer. I was growing in the faith, in my knowledge of the Word, and in my understanding of my ability to partner with God through prayer. I was learning that my Shepherd was not only still with me in the darkest of times, but that His power to help me was greatly manifested because His strength was made perfect in my weakness (2 Corinthians 12:9).

I was becoming less distracted by the voices asking me: "Where is God in all of this?" Instead, I became more receptive to the voice of truth breaking through the chaos and confusion to remind me of His Word and assure me of His comforting presence. One of the greatest helps in recognizing the Shepherd's voice was realizing that He actually listens to mine. His voice is always consistent with His Word, and His ear is always waiting for me to cry out to Him so He can answer me (Isaiah 30:19). The more I cried out to Him, the more I received His guidance; but the most perplexing difficulties of my career were still ahead of me.

CHAPTER 5

Shaped by a Condemned Inmate

God has never spoken to me in an audible voice nor by any private special revelation. However, He speaks to me constantly through His Word. He has brought to my memory passages of Scripture that I had read or heard while enabling me to realize that those very words of Scripture were unfolding and coming to life before my eyes in prison experiences. My faith in God grew stronger because of each of those experiences, both in challenging trials as well as in times of blessings.

I understood that God did not need human validation to make His Word true, and that He is still God, whether humans validate Him or not. I learned, however, that throughout biblical history, God chose to validate His Word for our sake. From His resurrection from the dead, to proving His power to forgive sins by healing the paralytic, to the showdown on Mount Carmel, our Lord repeatedly validated His Word for His people throughout history, and I discovered that He continues to do the same today.

Although faith is the evidence of things unseen, and believers must walk by faith, not by sight, the Holy Spirit authenticates the truth of the Gospel as very much alive and active through and for the witness of His Church. God always spoke to my heart while I read or listened to His Word, but He would set my heart ablaze when He regularly validated His Word through my experiences. The Bible says that His Word is alive and active, and I witnessed His Word being lived out in front of my face, or validated, countless times. The most common validation of God's Word came in the form of His grace to "the least of these." I was endlessly working and praying hard to remember that God loved the inmates every bit as much as He loved me. Even though I failed constantly, I knew that following God's instruction to be as innocent as a dove meant that I needed to love the inmates with the same grace God was giving me.

The Lord helped me grow in this kind of love by allowing me to personally witness some of the meanest, most heartless, dangerous criminals be completely transformed by the Gospel. My heart remembered what God's Word told us about Paul: "'He who used to persecute us is now preaching the faith he once tried to destroy.' And they glorified God because of me" (Galatians 1:23–24). My experiences validated that Word when certain inmates whom I knew to be cold-hearted criminals were enabled and empowered to transform completely, love the Lord with all of their heart, and not only preach the Word but live the Word with gentleness and grace. I saw human wolves—who once preyed upon others—grow to love and care for others with a godly passion (Isaiah 11:6; 65:25). Only God could ever possibly work such a work in a human heart, and I saw this happen numerous times.

[X] From Wolf to Sheep

One of the most profound examples of this work of God was a certain human wolf who was not only transformed to be a sheep of His flock, but also became such a strong follower of the Good Shepherd that I learned a lot from this living witness. In over 150 inmate execution experiences, there is one that clearly stood out as the most profound and personally significant of my career. It helped shape the direction of my mind and the condition of my heart. God caused His Word to come to life countless times through this singular experience. This event was the execution of Karla Faye Tucker. The impact of that evening weighed heavier on me than anything I can recall in my life.

When I came home that night, after the task was finally over, my wife said that she had never seen me act that way before. I couldn't describe my feelings to her for a long while. It was the only execution I ever had to "recover from." I found myself needing to block out everything else from my mind and just sink deeply into a long, quiet contemplation to reflect on all that I had witnessed and been through.

This is death row inmate Karla Faye Tucker. Karla was the first woman to be executed in the United States since 1984 and the first in Texas since 1863. She was transformed in prison from "wolf" to "sheep" and became a powerful witness for Christ.

Photo courtesy of Ron Kuntz.

Karla Faye Tucker sat on death row for approximately fourteen years after committing an extremely violent double murder for which she never claimed innocence or denied. In 1983, Karla was a twenty-three-year-old prostitute and drug addict when she plunged a pickaxe at least twenty times into the bodies of her two victims. When her crime scene was discovered, one of the victims still had the pickaxe embedded in her chest. At her capital murder trial, she proudly described to the jurors how she had not only killed her victims but also enjoyed doing so. Even when she came to prison, in her earliest days behind bars, she was a defiant and manipulative convict. Karla Faye Tucker was a wolf. Somewhere in those first years of her incarceration, however, the message of the Gospel had broken through her defenses and penetrated her heart, setting her life on a new and different course. She had become a sheep.

When Karla arrived at our unit from the female death row, I had never seen her before or heard anything about her other than that she was scheduled to be the first female executed in Texas since 1863. I had heard Chaplain Brazzil comment that she was a strong Christian, but we have had many death row inmates come here to the death house as converted and strong Christians, so I wasn't prepared for all that I was about to witness.

There was an ocean of media coverage outside the Walls Unit and an ever-growing mob of thousands of spectators and protestors surrounding our unit, so we were all in a mode of extra-tight security; but I didn't let that get to me. In addition, Karla's physical appearance—so small and fragile-looking—was definitely different and strange to all of us on the death squad; but that wasn't what affected me either.

We have executed many inmates who have touched me with their conversion and their serious faith in Jesus, but Karla was different—tremendously different. When Jim Brazzil introduced her to me and I shook her hand, I quickly noticed that she had an unusually high degree of peace about her for someone about to be executed. As I conversed with her for a while, then stood back and observed her interacting with others, I was increasingly impressed with how relaxed and comfortable she was, which is very unusual for a condemned inmate in the final hours of life. As I continued to observe her behavior, it became completely clear that she was indeed full of the joy of the Lord and showed no signs of the typical fear and anxiety we normally see. She never got preachy or overly verbal about her faith, but the fruit of the Spirit shining through her behavior and countenance was giving a louder testimony and a more effective witness than any words.

Veterans of prison management have become experts to some extent at detecting phony, con man games and fake, empty portrayals by inmates pretending to be Christians in an effort to gain our trust. On this evening, however, even the most skeptical of scoffers had no question or doubt that Karla's faith in God was genuine and real. We saw none of the frequently seen practice of inmates using their "relationship with God" to draw attention to themselves or gain sympathy. She was definitely in a position to orchestrate or command sympathy and pity from millions, but we never saw evidence of that in her. Karla was center-stage to the world on that day, but she chose to give up that position and give it to Jesus. Rather than making this her moment to shine, she reflected Him and allowed His light to shine. Instead of drawing attention to herself, Karla was steadily ministering to everyone around her with serious, loving concern, not false piety. When the food servers brought her last meal into her cell, she deeply edified their work and praised the quality of their efforts with such enthusiasm that it made their day and literally raised their self-image. I was completely amazed at the power of God in her to impact and bless others.

Some of the female death row officers were there with us, and you could tell they really loved Karla, making this duty a difficult burden for them. Karla showed intense concern for their sadness and the discomfort all of this was causing them. The closer it came to 6:00 p.m., the more upset the female guards became, but Karla kept telling them, "Don't worry, you're going to be okay, you're going to be all right."

Watching this condemned inmate console, comfort, and minister to her keepers was completely amazing to me. If anyone in that death house had a reason to be crying, it was the inmate herself; but Karla was genuinely concerned for the well-being of others and was very effectively ministering to them. Karla never wanted any pity or sympathy, nor did she want the attention for herself; rather, she was attentive never to miss an opportunity to bless an employee or visitor with encouraging words of appreciation and to compliment them. I don't recall any other condemned inmates thanking us for taking such good care of them and being so nice to them, but she regularly thanked us for our "kindness."

Karla's prayer time that day was spent praying for others, not for herself. Her prayers reminded me of how a mother will make absolutely sure that her children are completely well-fed before she dare take a bite for herself, or that her kids have new clothes and new shoes while she wears the same old ones. Karla was serving and giving of herself as if it were just a normal day for her. She wore a smile all day, and not a weak smile either; she exuded real joyful and genuine happiness. She was not only in a positive mood that evening, but she even occasionally laughed and showed excitement. Her attitude and actions caught us all totally off guard. Her focus was on Jesus, and she allowed Him to use her to heavily influence us all. Most inmates consider us the enemy. Karla Faye Tucker considered us a "mission field" and an opportunity for outreach.

In one of my pastor's sermons, he give a powerful statement that helps me put this into words. He said:

> *Showing love for those who love us is nice, but normal. Showing love for the oppressed is far too uncommon, but is touching and admirable. The rarest and the most amazing expression of love, however, is love for our enemies.*

When prisoners sincerely love their jailers, even their executioners, that's God's love! It's not earned. It's not deserved. It's grace. That type of love is baffling and overwhelming to our carnal minds. I saw this dramatically lived out during the execution of Karla Faye Tucker. God's love enveloped us through her that day, and we were indeed embraced, overcome, and overwhelmed by that love!

Love isn't something commonly felt in a prison, but we felt a powerful love inside the death house that night. At the exact same time outside of the prison, however, there were some who were feeling the opposite. Approximately half of the crowd in front of our prison did not care if she had been transformed from her old ways, and many refused to believe that she was really a Christian at all. Some were shouting that she was faking her Christianity to gain sympathy. They accused her of being a wolf in sheep's clothing. All converted criminals have a hard time shaking the reputation of their past. Many born-again Christians have to live with the uncomfortable knowledge that some hearts will never forgive them. Karla wasn't disheartened by those who still saw her as a wolf, nor did she allow them to steal the focus of her heart.

Many today will remember hearing on news channels about Christian leaders all over the world insisting that Karla's life should be spared because she was no longer the same person who had committed that crime. Numerous religious leaders were adamant that she had been reborn into a new creation and was an entirely changed and different person. I had no problem believing any of that, but on the evening of her execution, I never saw any signs of Karla being overly concerned about fighting for her freedom or losing her life. There was indeed such a tremendous plea and fight raged by countless others across the country and the world on her behalf that we weren't even sure if this execution would actually go through or not. What did come through to me loud and clear, however, was that while people all over the world were pleading for her pardon through the governor, her focus was on her pardon through Jesus, which she knew she had already received.

Whether Christian or not, everyone who came into the death house that day left with a complete understanding that her uncanny strength and peace were coming from her great faith in God. This was a powerful witness because many knew that Karla had a power within her that they did not have. I'm sure that most of the staff realized the same thing I perceived—that the one who was supposed to be the most powerless person in this picture was unquestionably the most powerful! There was actually a very reverent atmosphere in the death house throughout the day because of her attitude and the way she treated everyone. On that day, God used Karla Faye Tucker to transform the death house into a church house. I found myself being taught and mentored by the behavior of a condemned criminal from death row!

☒ The Witness of an Inmate

I went from being impressed by her faith to asking myself:

- *Is there that much visible evidence of Christ in my life?*
- *Do my thoughts and words exemplify a Christian heart that well?*
- *Do others see Jesus in my actions?*
- *Do I stay this focused on Christ during my hard times?*

I was humbled to concede that the answer to these questions was a definite no!

This was the first inmate whom my heart truly accepted as a real brother or sister in Christ. Much more than that, this ex-wolf was a teaching instrument in the hand of God to gently give me a major dose of humbling that I desperately needed.

The account of the "sinful woman" described in Luke 7:36–47 came to life. Jesus explained that those who are forgiven little, love little, but those who are forgiven much, love much. Karla's crime was horrible; but her transformed love for God and her fellow man was that of someone massively appreciative of being forgiven much. The Bible teaches us in Romans 4:7–8: "Blessed are those whose lawless deeds are forgiven, and whose sins are covered; blessed is the man against whom the Lord will not count his sin."

Karla knew that her worst and ugliest sins were covered and would never be counted against her. She knew that she was blessed. Her remarkable display of confidence in the middle of a crisis was a faith witness not only uncommon among condemned inmates in their final hours, but far too uncommon among us "free-world" Christians as well. God only knows how many people left the death house that day seeking and desiring to know Jesus or know Him better because of an insuppressible conviction in their souls. I believe that many went home that night desperately wanting and hungering for the peace, confidence, and assurance that Karla had. She may very well have performed a far more powerful witness in her death than she ever could have in a long, full life — in or out of prison.

The strength Karla demonstrated was far greater than herself and not possible without a strong indwelling of the Holy Spirit. It is extremely difficult for inmates to overcome the loss of credibility that naturally occurs when they put on those white uniforms. For her to simply earn the respect of her keepers was a rare milestone, but to wield the sword of the Spirit so effectively over so many in this particular kind of audience was unquestionably a "God thing."

Karla's witness amazed my heart and convicted my soul, but I was imagining that all of this could have been even more mind-boggling to anyone there who may have been completely unchurched. If anyone present that day was viewing this from a strictly humanistic perspective, he must have been asking himself, "What's wrong with this girl? Doesn't she even care that she is about to die?"

The truth was that Karla had already died "to self" and was therefore more concerned with following Jesus and serving others than with any of her present personal circumstances. It takes solid Christian maturity to remain focused on the fact that even in our darkest hour, a saved child of God has more blessings to rejoice over than sufferings to cry about. God made His Word in Philippians come alive right in front of me. The apostle Paul was nearing the time of his own execution when he wrote the following passages:

> *For to me to live is Christ, and to die is gain. If I am to live in the flesh, that means fruitful labor for me. Yet which I shall choose I cannot tell. I am hard pressed between the two. My desire is to depart and be with Christ, for that is far better. (1:21–23)*

Do nothing from selfish ambition or conceit, but in humility count others more significant than yourselves. Let each of you look not only to his own interests, but also to the interests of others. Have this mind among yourselves, which is yours in Christ Jesus. (2:3–5)

I remember thinking that Karla's final few hours were such an impressive exhibit of the Great Commandment in action (Matthew 22:37–39) in action, that my life should display that kind of concern for others if my heart is truly full of love for God and neighbor. The evening was slightly longer than normal, but the process followed its course that night. The petite body of Karla Faye Tucker was strapped to the gurney, and we all assumed our positions and awaited her last statement. Her last words were exactly like her actions that day, not preachy or showy; rather, she just apologized for her crime, then thanked, edified, and loved her family and the prison staff. She told the prison staff, "I love all of you very much. You've been so good to me." Then she went to be with Jesus.

☒ Peace that Passes All Understanding

Karla was still an inspiration to those of us in the death house even after she was gone, because all believers knew that she was with the Lord, as we all want to be. While she was still running the good race and fighting the good fight, she knew she would someday hear those precious words of Jesus that all believers long to hear: "Well done, good and faithful servant" (Matthew 25:23).

No one denied that this executed inmate was a murderer, but Jesus said, "I tell you, there will be more joy in heaven over one sinner who repents than over ninety-nine righteous persons who need no repentance" (Luke 15:7). She had accepted the consequences of her crime and did not grieve as those who have no hope (1 Thessalonians 4:13). God's Word tells us that "precious in the sight of the LORD is the death of His saints" (Psalm 116:15). Since the very first time I read that verse, my mind has tried to grasp an image of Jesus up in heaven personally and attentively watching each believer as they leave this life in the death of their earthly body. As I watched Karla Faye Tucker die, my ability to see an image of the reality of that Scripture verse became a little clearer.

God used Karla's life as a powerful example of His message that, though we are all guilty of some ugly sins and must face the consequences in this life, "we are more than conquerors" in the final, purposeful big picture, thanks to the awesome redeeming love and atoning sacrifice of Jesus Christ (Romans 8:37; Job 19:25–26). How comforting and exciting it is to know that we, too, can be forgiven of absolutely anything because Jesus' blood is more powerful than our worst faults and biggest obstacles in this life (1 John 2:1–2). Coming from such a very dark place earlier in her life, Karla's witness was an exceptionally bright light for Christ.

That night, the entire death squad left very quietly and somber-ly—more so than ever before. Chaplain Jim Brazzil had never been so inundated with staff needing counsel in an attempt to understand why this execution affected them so severely. Many "tough" death squad veterans were having a hard time sorting this one out in their heads and in their hearts. Although I would like to say I was a pillar of Christian strength and stability, I was so humbled by Karla's witness that my only strength was that which the Lord was providing one min-ute at a time. It took me a good while to soak it all in. On that execu-tion evening, there was none of the usual tumultuous struggle tugging my heart in different directions; instead, I felt a profound peace that passes all understanding. It was a strangely emotional day that was dif-ficult to explain and describe.

Over the days and weeks that followed Karla's execution, I was able to collect my thoughts and recognize how many times God had caused me to witness His Word come to life during that event. Most of those instances were revelations that personally humbled me. As I analyzed that experience, I realized that Karla loved much because she was so seriously aware of how much she had been forgiven. I began to realize that I needed to be like her in that regard. My sins were many and the trail of victims from people I had hurt was probably a longer list than Karla's. This awareness was finally driving me to my knees in a daily repentant posture of humility before God that I crucially needed. I was slowly getting the picture that my greatest weaknesses had been pride and self-righteousness, which necessarily called for ongoing life lessons to chip away at the icy wall that pride had built around my heart. The thawing of my heart was a painful and embarrassingly slow process, but I knew God was steadily shaping me because my compassion for those I once loathed was increasing.

CHAPTER 6

Shaped by Prison Ministry Workers

I was both humbled and blessed to realize that Karla Faye Tucker, a convicted murderer, had a far better grasp on grace and a much greater faith walk than I did. I was determined not to waste those lessons the Lord allowed me to learn. My faith walk changed from a primary focus on merely studying God's Word to having an equally heavy focus on living His Word by serving Christ and others. Thankfully, that change in focus caused the more desperately needed growth in the condition of my heart. When my heart was moved to be less self-centered—I went from simply being available for service to having an intense eagerness to serve—I felt closer to the Lord. I more clearly and frequently felt His prompting to join Him where He was at work in the people all around me. I began to recognize and respond to needs I hadn't noticed before. There was a greater war going on in the prison than I had previously understood.

Quite often my job was a ringside, front-row seat to observe some of the most vicious and heated spiritual battles anyone could witness. I saw firsthand the intense efforts of the devil to steal, kill, and destroy lives that were created to know and love God. I was not excluded from his hit list. Satan never tired of trying to snatch me away from the purpose God had for me. The enemy had succeeded in derailing me in the beginning of my career, and I knew that only constant prayer would protect me from falling off track again.

☒ Law and Gospel; Justice and Mercy

In answer to my prayers, God taught me a profound lesson one day when I walked into the officer's dining room to take my lunch break.

After filling my tray at the cafeteria-style buffet line, I sat down at a table where a co-worker of mine and a prison ministry worker were seated. They were discussing an incident at another prison where some guards had been accused of mistreatment of an inmate and excessive use of force in quelling a disturbance. After a few minutes, my co-worker left the dining room to return to work and left me sitting there with the prison ministry worker.

This man was probably in his seventies and had a very gentle, joyful disposition. He was a frequent visitor to our unit, and I knew him to be a wise and very experienced man. Therefore, when he asked me if I was familiar with the incident, I vulnerably shared my feelings. I told him yes, and admitted that I once had an attitude and behavior similar to what those officers were being accused of. I explained that by a miracle straight from God I was delivered from the biggest part of my old character many years ago, and I was praying daily about the many rough edges I still had. I further explained that I was committed to following the Lord and never returning to my old ways, but that I had an ongoing serious struggle with my emotions tugging my heart in different directions.

I told him that I had witnessed the vast majority of prison employees fall into one of two categories: hating inmates or becoming too close to them. Even though I never intended to fall into either trap, the things I witnessed in prison regularly tugged my heart toward one or the other of those two directions. I wanted to please God with my decisions and reactions to each crisis, but my emotions often lured me in conflicting directions so that I was not always certain of the appropriate Christian response.

The minister leaned forward with his elbows on the table, his chin resting on his clasped hands. He slowly began to nod his head as if in agreement with me. He acted as though he were in deep contemplation of my words for a moment; then he taught me something that would become another priceless habit I would follow for the rest of my career.

He said: "All of us are bent toward a certain type of sinful habit with which we struggle. The biggest difference between us and these prison inmates is that the sinful habits with which they struggle are the type that makes them too dangerous to live among others out in the free world. Some are deemed too dangerous to remain living at all."

Then he slowly turned his head to the left, looked at an inmate, raised his voice just a little, and said: "Isn't that right?"

This inmate was working in food services, busy replenishing the buffet line about forty feet away with his back turned to us, but he answered as if he had been part of the conversation all along.

"Yes, sir, they know better than to ever let me out of here." The inmate then snickered as if embarrassed to be caught eavesdropping, gathered his pans, and disappeared behind the serving line and into the kitchen.

"Pray for him," the prison minister told me. "He does not really struggle with his sin problem because he loves it so much."

He continued: "I have often imagined the challenge it must be for correctional officers and peace officers who really love the Lord. You have a serious responsibility to protect society from dangerous criminals, but you have an equally serious responsibility to love the predatory offenders. I love these inmates with all of my heart, but I do not have your daily duty to keep them from killing one another in here and innocent people out there. I have a lot of respect for those of you who answer God's call to do both. The problem you are struggling with is actually a mirror of a very common problem in the church. There are two inappropriate extremes of thinking, and many Christians drift off into one or the other. One side believes that being a Christian means to be unconditionally loving, forgiving, and tolerant of all types of sin and sinners. The other side believes that being a Christian means to be rigidly intolerant of all sin and sinners."

He went on: "Our job is to regularly study God's Word so that we know enough about His heart and His will to walk in a proper balance of Law and Gospel, justice and mercy." Then he stood up, wiped his face with his napkin, and walked toward the door to leave the dining room. Just before disappearing into the hallway, he paused, turned toward me, and with a big grin on his face, said: "This is a wonderful problem if it keeps you constantly studying God's Word for the answers." Then he gave me a thumbs-up and walked out. His words were very closely aligned with Dr. Beto's counsel to me years before. God obviously wanted me to hear a similar message but a little more pointed.

As I contemplated his comments, I was comforted to realize that the constant tug-of-war for the convictions of my heart could actually be a blessing if I kept my eyes on Jesus. My struggle to discern right from wrong in every situation was appropriate. It was right to have a deep yearning to learn and follow God's will in matters where I was uncertain. It took years, however, for me to trust God enough to allow Him to realign my heart with His Word and away from my own wavering emotions.

It took a while for me to understand that criminal justice public servants were not a necessary evil, but a necessary good. It remained a long and difficult struggle of discerning truth from lies before I confidently knew that I was not compromising my commitment and service to God by being deeply committed to my professional duty of serving the government. Likewise, I eventually became confident that I was not compromising my duty by feeling heavy compassion for inmates when I filtered my feelings through God's Word.

Satan caused hundreds of tugs-of-war in my heart, but God caused every battle to work together for good as He enabled me to navigate through each storm, learning a little bit more about His heart and His will every time.

I once heard my pastor say that God wins every spiritual battle over Satan when people ask for and receive God's grace every time they slip and fall. The problem, my pastor explained, is that even though Satan is actually a prowling lion, seeking whom he may devour, his lies are enticing enough to lure many to follow him until they are completely consumed. In my heart, I knew my pastor was right, because all of us feel the pain and suffering caused by the devil's attacks. But I saw many who never realized they were in his jaws until their lives had been destroyed. I understood that Satan was the controlling force inside every human wolf that preyed upon others. I personally learned the hard way that the grip of Satan on a deceived heart is powerful and destructive, but the transforming power of Jesus is far more powerful. I have also seen many lives clutched in the jaws of the enemy so severely that I was guilty of giving up all hope for their souls. God, however, rescued me from that element of disbelief by allowing me to witness many condemned inmates receiving God's grace in Jesus Christ as their Lord and Savior in the last hours of their lives.

X Spiritual Battlefields

On one calm and memorable execution night, the crowd of protestors was unusually small and quiet. The two witnessing families—the relatives of the inmate and the relatives of the inmate's victim—appeared peaceful and self-controlled. A reasonably low-key atmosphere like this on an execution night is a rare blessing for everyone involved. I am always thankful when this happens, especially for the sake of the families at the death house. Their struggle to deal with the execution seemed strangely less intense than the war we usually see raging within them.

On this particular night, it was obvious to me that the witnessing families were already blessed with the grace of answered prayer. The more I spoke with them, the more clearly I saw that they were Christians with a strong, confident faith. They indisputably had the hand of God protecting them from the enemy's efforts and desire to torment them with this normally stressful process. As I gave thanks for the Lord's hand upon these relaxed and comforted people, I recalled all of the many witnesses from previous executions who had not been delivered from their battles with the enemy. Thank God that this particular night was proceeding with an encouraging peacefulness.

As I escorted the procession back to the death house, the atmosphere was so relaxed that my mind gave way to the luxury of drifting to some other thoughts for a few moments. I was recalling some other people I had encountered earlier that day who were deeply entrenched in ugly battles with the forces of Satan.

First, I had an inmate in my office who had half his body tattooed in satanic and demonic symbols, while the other half was covered with tattoos of various Christian symbols. When I spoke with the guy, I could tell that he was fighting just as much of a crazy, confused war in his heart and spirit as was reflected in the graphics all over his skin.

Then, on my break, while driving across town and listening to our local Christian radio station, I heard the DJ say: "Okay, prayer warriors, we're going to take some prayer requests! . . . Hello . . . Do you have a prayer request?" The slow-speaking voice of a man who sounded very tired and defeated came over the phone. The poor fellow groaned and sighed, then said, "My wife is in the hospital with cancer, and the doctors aren't giving her much time. We have two small children who are full of questions that I don't know how to answer, and our kids just . . . really don't understand what's happening here. Please pray for my kids to make it through this." I was having a tough time driving after that call, as my eyes filled with tears and a huge lump formed in my throat. I could tell the DJ was affected as well, as she said, "Thank you for calling, sir. Prayer warriors, please lift up this man, his wife, and their children in prayer."

Then she took another one: "Hello . . . Do you have a prayer request?" This time a little girl's voice came over the phone. I guessed from the voice that she must have been nine or ten years old. She was crying as she spoke. She said, "Please pray for my daddy! My daddy has run away and he won't come home, and my mommy is scared and crying, and I'm scared, and we don't know what to do! Please pray for my daddy!"

The pain and anguish these people were feeling underneath the crushing weight of Satan's oppression was ripping my heart to pieces! I had tears streaming down my face, and my spirit was aching for them as I drove. I was so overwhelmed, I couldn't stand it anymore. I pulled over to the side of the road, got out of my car and fell to my knees right there, crying out to God in loud, intercessory prayer for these poor brothers and sisters to somehow be relieved from the casualties of the battle the enemy was waging against them.

The memory of those hurting callers, asking for prayer, was causing another huge lump in my throat as I was leading the witnesses down to the execution viewing area. My mind was still reflecting on the earlier encounters of that day and God was helping me to realize that the contest of good versus evil rages everywhere. I was learning that the hearts and lives of all people are potential battlefields for the constant waging of spiritual war. Some battle zones look particularly fierce and bloody while others seem to be enjoying occasional cease-fires. And to discourage me, Satan, "the father of lies," would have me believe that he is winning.

When I focused more on the enemy's evidence than on the truth of God's Word, I could easily become discouraged and seduced into believing that some battles are already lost and not worth fighting. After all, it is easy to view the state penitentiary as a prisoner of war camp full of the lives that Satan has won at least temporary victory over. Death row certainly appears to be a trophy case where the prince of darkness proudly displays those lives over which he has won a permanent victory. What I have seen in the death chamber on execution nights, however, bears witness that death row produces some of the most exciting and joyous victories for Jesus Christ.

As I arrived at the viewing room of the death house, my mind returned to the task at hand. I escorted the witnesses to their places, then gave the signal that we were all ready. I glanced at my watch; it was 6:15 p.m. We were right on schedule. The condemned inmate was strapped securely to the death gurney with the IV in his arm, and all witnesses stood, watching the warden as he asked, "Do you have any last words?"

What transpired over the next five minutes was one of the most awesome witnesses of a relationship between a mortal human being and the eternal God that anyone will ever see. The inmate was smiling from ear to ear with a sparkle in his eye like a kid on Christmas morning. From the expression on his face, you would have thought he had just won a million dollars or that his favorite team had just won the Super Bowl. I can see him as clearly now as if it just happened yesterday, and I will never forget him or his countenance.

The inmate spoke, not to any of us, but directly to Jesus. I got the impression that he was looking directly into Jesus' eyes. His voice was ecstatic! He kept saying, "Here I come, Jesus! Thank you for saving me, Jesus! I love you, Lord!" over and over. He wasn't just ready to go—he was deliriously excited. He was like a child who had been waiting all day long and his daddy was finally home. I looked up to heaven, and under my breath I asked God to please help me to be this ready when my hour comes to go home. Admittedly, I was envious.

Nothing in the world could possibly compare with the feeling of knowing that you've run the race, fought the good fight, and reached the ultimate goal! To know that you're seconds away from being with the Lord and spending eternity in His presence must create uncontainable excitement. The rest of us don't know our day or hour, and we all have to keep running our races and fighting the temptations to occasionally make wrong choices and slip into the sin that so easily entangles us (Hebrews 12:1). When the inmate finally told the warden, "Okay, I'm ready!" it was as if to say, "Hurry up! I've been waiting all my life for this moment." As the lethal injection took effect, and it was obvious that he had died, I was imagining this guy with the Lord. I was sure that as soon as he saw them, he would probably be giving a high-five to the angels and leaping into Jesus' arms. I found myself thinking that I couldn't wait to see this guy again.

I don't believe those favored to witness this dramatic departure had any doubt that the inmate had gone from this earth into the presence of the living God. There was no question about who had won the battle. The enemy called Satan obviously caused this inmate to stumble earlier in his life, but ultimately the trophy went to Jesus. After witnessing that execution experience, I never again asked the Lord how capital punishment could possibly be in the best interest of the condemned inmate. The Lord clearly showed me that if a death sentence and pending execution becomes the vehicle that drives a condemned inmate to Christ and saves him or her from hell, it is the biggest blessing of that person's life.

The truth is that there are many death row inmates who are actually glad and feel blessed to be there. Those are the ones who have received God's grace and become believers in prison. They know that if they had continued down the destructive paths they were on out in the free world, they most likely would have died there, lost in their sins. Many condemned inmates are grateful that death row was their opportunity to escape their former way of life. Death row was the circumstance God used to enable their hearts to hear the Gospel, receive God's grace, and follow Jesus as their Lord and Savior.

Death row is not, however, an easy battlefield. There are casualties. Of course, not all executions end in salvation. It is often an ugly and even grotesque combat zone where the inmates' hearts and souls fight long and hard between good and evil for years and even decades. When an inmate is sentenced to death and arrives at death row, it is usually at the culmination of an entire lifetime of entanglement in the enemy's web of deceitfulness.

The murder committed that results in this consequence is often the product of a hardened attitude of selfish indifference and a callous disregard for the feelings of others. Worse yet, it may be a product of bitterness toward self and hatefulness toward others, including God. A person firmly entrenched in such an attitude formed over a lifetime will not be changed overnight and is resistant to anyone's advice or suggestion for change. Some inmates are so angry with all the people and conditions they blame for their predicament that they have seemingly impenetrable shells around their hearts.

Others, once given time to face reality, do admit that their own bad choices caused them to do wrong. In their brokenness, they are open to ideas for personal change. In many instances, broken is good! A person who has been broken is extremely fertile ground for being rebuilt by the truth. It has been aptly said that some things are worthless *when* they are broken, but other things are worthless *until* they are broken.

Many inmates are indeed reached on death row by prison ministry workers sent by God to sow His truth into their lives. The fruit of the labors of these ministers is evident and plentiful. Many inmates are so grateful for receiving new life in Christ that they refer to their death row cell as "life row"! The value of the men and women who sacrificially and willingly give their lives in prison ministry is tremendous. Whether they are a small outreach from a local church or part of a huge prison ministry, their value is indeed priceless.

☒ "Hug-a-Thug"

I am not exaggerating when I say that prison ministry workers "give their lives" to prison work. Prison ministry is not something someone can just lightly dabble with or experiment in as some kind of hobby. For the few who answer this call, it is an all-consuming, passionate, life-changing decision. This is an extraordinarily difficult mission field. These inmates are more than just tough shells to crack spiritually; they can also be extremely dangerous. We once had a prison ministry worker whose arm was pulled through the cell bars on death row and slashed to pieces by the one he was trying to help. After many years of working in the state penitentiary, I came to see these workers as sheep ministering to wolves or lambs trying to help lions.

Imagine yourself as a brand-new prison ministry volunteer, walking up to the front gate of the state penitentiary. Your ears work just fine. You can distinctly hear the din of what sounds like a war coming from the inside. Your eyes work just fine. You can clearly see the towering walls of steel, brick, barbed wire, and razor wire encircling the compound. You see many gun towers, manned by heavily armed and stern-faced guards, all around the perimeter. Everything is designed to protect you from the inhabitants of this place; yet you ignore all of that and walk right in among them. You approach the front gate and read a sign on the fence that states:

WARNING!
IN THE EVENT THAT YOU SHOULD BE TAKEN HOSTAGE, YOUR LIFE WILL *NOT* BE BARGAINED FOR.

At this point, if you keep walking inside the prison, you are either crazy or you're crazy about Jesus and will stop at nothing to share the feeling! Prison ministry actually does defy the logic of normal human thinking, but then, picking up your cross and following Jesus always does. To overcome all of these obstacles and still answer the call to volunteer for prison ministry is a miraculous blessing straight from God.

Earlier in my career, I viewed prison ministry workers as gullible and naïve. I lived with the inmates every day. I knew their con games and their manipulative tactics. I knew that typical inmates are experts at deceit and can't be trusted. Many inmates display a worse character inside the prison than they did out in the free world. On a routine basis, I saw inmates prey upon and abuse one another and defy and abuse the guards.

I knew that any inmates who truly wanted to change their behavior or respond to the Holy Spirit's tug on their heart had two dark clouds hanging overhead, following them everywhere: their own past behavior (their crime) and the behavior of the other inmates around them. Both of these inhibit the ability to achieve personal credibility. Because so many acts of remorse, repentance, or humility on the part of an inmate are eventually proven to be manipulative, most prison employees view all "religious" inmates as simply playing a game.

With all of this in mind, you can imagine how receptive we guards were to free-world prison ministry workers as they came into the prison. We had a nickname for those who entered the prison to minister to inmates: we called them "Hug-a-Thug" people.

It took a long time, but I gradually overcame my suspicion and distrust of these volunteers. I came to realize that they are truly some of those who follow the example of the Good Shepherd in John 10. There we read that a hired hand cares nothing for the sheep and will run away when he sees a wolf coming, but the Good Shepherd loves the sheep and will lay down His life for them. Prisons are mission fields abundantly ripe for harvesting souls, but the workers are indeed too few. I thank God for each and every "Hug-a-Thug" minister; without them, the spiritual casualties would be astronomical.

☒ The Final Showdown

Unfortunately, God's ministers are not the only influence offered to those on death row. As warned in 1 Peter 5:8, our adversary, the devil, definitely roams and patrols there, seeking whom he may devour. The evil enemy is very active on death row, and the battle for souls rages persistently and aggressively. Inmates are offered the most heinous of antidotes for their problems from a wide variety of false gods and false religions. Tragically, numerous people and groups work hard to prevent the inmates' brokenness and rebirth in the truth by supporting them with cleverly devised sympathy and justifications for their behavior. But sometimes, this only makes inmates more bitter, resentful, blaming, and rebellious. Many inmates hold firm to their anger and rejection of the truth right to the very end.

The last few hours of many people's lives in the death house culminate in a final showdown of good versus evil. In Texas, for many years, God's main weapon chosen for this showdown was Chaplain Jim Brazzil. Jim had a gentle character and tremendous patience and compassion. Jim would sit with the condemned inmates for their last six hours of life. He comforted and consoled them and was their true friend during this time. Chaplain Brazzil was the primary reason most executions took place peacefully and without much anxiety or

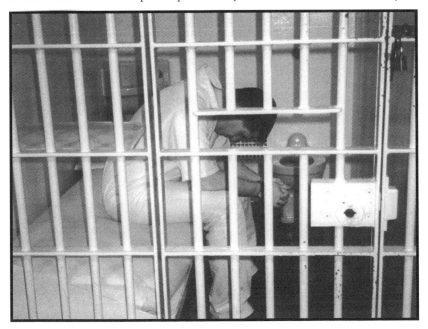

This is the death house holding cell where death row inmates spend the final hours of their lives.

resistance. Jim was there to offer the truth to these men in the hopes that they would receive it. Jim introduced me to many inmates in that holding cell just outside the death chamber who had, just at that moment, received the grace of God and now believed the Gospel and were clinging to Jesus Christ in faith. What a blessing to have the privilege of ushering once-doomed souls to heaven, thwarting Satan's plans to receive them to eternal damnation.

Jim was a priceless brother in Christ to me, but to the inmates, he was the most relatable prison ministry worker I had ever seen. He never treated an inmate like an inmate, but rather as a true friend. Whenever I was present for an inmate chapel service that Jim was leading, I could easily forget that it was a prison service. From his sermons to his music to his prayer times, he would speak as if he were addressing a free-world congregation, not convicts who needed reha-bilitating. The inmates trusted and loved Jim, and he loved them. Jim knew that his congregation came from every background imaginable and he related to all of them. It was obvious that Jim's placement as the death house chaplain was certainly a divine appointment. What these condemned inmates needed most in the final hours of their lives was the love of Jesus Christ, who manifested Himself to them through the instrument of Chaplain Brazzil. I've seen numerous con-demned men transformed from despair, defeat, and hopelessness to joy, relief, and assurance of salvation in Jesus through the Gospel of Jesus Christ delivered by Jim Brazzil.

There is no more exhilarating experience than to shake a con-demned man's hand in congratulations and share the joy of his new-found peace and freedom in Jesus. It is indescribably exciting to feel his relief and see the happiness in his eyes, especially when I am so completely aware that we'll be grabbing this same hand in a short time to load his cold, lifeless body into a hearse . . . but he won't be there, he'll be with Jesus.

I've heard many people argue that people can't live in sinful re-bellion all their lives, then turn and be saved in the last few minutes

Some death row inmates spend the final hours of their lives using this holding cell as a sanctuary for deep, intimate fellowship with Jesus Christ.

of life. But Jesus' words to the thief on the cross next to Him tell us all that, until we die, it's never too late to receive Jesus (Luke 23:39–43). Our Lord told the parable of the workers in the vineyard (Matthew 20:1–16) to teach us that, whether converted early in life or late in life, no one deserves or earns God's grace and mercy. It is a gift that is continuously offered right up to our final hour.

How do we deal with human wolves? I learned that one of the most important ways is to treat them with a heart of ministry. If our Lord is persistently patient with even the most wicked, not wanting them to perish in eternal destruction, we must have the same heart. Jesus gives a personal invitation to those whose time is short: "While you have the light, believe in the light" (John 12:36). This offer from our Lord also comes with a warning that the window of opportunity does end at death. Although some who are not on death row might think they have more time, Jesus makes it clear that anyone's day could be finished before they are finished with their day!

X Hearts of Mercy

I never let my guard down or forgot the dangers of dealing with convicted murderers, but thanks to the influence of prison ministry workers, I learned that my primary obligation in dealing with human wolves was to have a heart of mercy. In the parable of the unmerciful servant, Jesus warned me not to let myself become unmerciful. His life on earth was an example of how to be merciful, and I certainly struggled with that call. It is worth whatever price we have to pay, however, to learn the fundamental lesson of mercy. In Matthew 5:7, Jesus declared, "Blessed are the merciful, for they shall receive mercy." My own need to obtain mercy should have been enough incentive to cause me to strive to be merciful. Accepting and embracing a fellow sinner as a new brother in Christ should have been the very least thing I could do in my answer to "the call." As I developed a more mature heart of greater mercy, I graduated to progressive degrees of showing compassion to both sheep and human wolves.

Those who are not called to prison ministry can still learn a great lesson by considering the merciful character modeled by prison ministry workers. A heart that truly cares about the lost or struggling condition of a fellow person and selflessly helps others to carry their burden is blessed indeed. When any of us devotedly give our time and efforts back to God for the strengthening of another soul during a season of weakness, we can rest assured that we, too, will see mercy whenever our strength is gone.

While working in the prison, I often became wearied with emotional burdens that drained all of my strength. I frequently retreated to my office, locked my door behind me, and fell to my knees before the Lord as I gave Him the burdens I could not handle.

By watching the faith in action of prison ministry workers, my heart developed a yearning to serve God by sharing the burdens of others. I quickly learned, however, that truly sharing another's burdens means submitting to the vulnerability of being weakened by that burden. God showed me that such service was a testimony of my trust that I, too, would obtain the mercy Jesus promised. I needed extra strength for those nights in the death house that were exceptionally depressing and negative. Occasionally, a condemned inmate would defiantly show and profess an outright hatred for God and reject Him to the bitter end. It is a cold and chilling feeling to watch a man pass from this life while cursing God and those of us who worked in the prison. Witnessing some people willingly choose eternal separation from God was sobering and sorrowful. It gave my heart an ever-greater hunger to draw closer to God and pursue Him more fervently.

Even in such ugly situations, however, God's justice and mercy was still the clear winner. After watching a condemned inmate openly reject God while dying, I asked a prison chaplain if losing the battle like that was discouraging to his efforts. He explained that one of God's most amazing gifts is that He allows His grace to be resistible. God never forces anyone to receive Him but does allow people to reject Him and choose eternal separation from Him. He further explained that in the battle of good versus evil, good wins every time. Sometimes, there is just no battle. When a person has chosen to completely reject good and there is no fight, God's justice is shown in the wages of the conscious choice to reject mercy and love. This explanation gave me a completely different perspective about the constant battles within my own heart. Because I was hungry to know the Truth, the differing perceptions of this world caused battles within me, but when I prayed and looked to the Shepherd, good won every time.

My regular encounters with prison ministry workers were used by God to shape my heart to be a little bit more like His. God used these ministers and their tenacious zeal to share the Gospel with "the least of these" as a priceless influence. Their desire to reach the lost and love the unlovable was so far beyond mine that I was constantly convicted and compelled to pray for the same heart. Their influence would prove to be a critical blessing from the Lord, because I would encounter numerous other influences that worked tirelessly to stunt my growth and shape my heart in a different direction.

CHAPTER 7

Shaped by Families of the Victims

Slowly but surely, the Lord helped me develop a bigger and better heart of ministry for hard-to-love human wolves. The one obstacle that probably stunted my growth the most, however, was the devil's ability to lure my heart into intense anger toward many death row inmates for all of the pain and suffering they caused to the families of their victims. My constant encounters with these families allowed me to see firsthand how many lives were completely devastated far beyond those of the actual murder victims themselves. The appropriate feelings of righteous anger against evil, injustice, and cruelty inappropriately tugged my heart back toward the condemning, self-righteous old me from whom I had prayed and worked so hard to escape. Satan continuously tempted me to return to an inappropriate personal zeal and pride of being an agent of God's wrath upon evil human wolves. Thankfully, God answered my endless prayers for protection and always allowed me to catch myself before I slipped too far in the wrong direction. As I write this chapter, I am praying for the protection of every reader's heart from this same temptation as I share the experiences in this stage of my transformation journey.

I have observed that the series of events following every capital murder is always the same. Upon discovery of the horrible crime, society is shocked and outraged. Everyone's anger and contempt is aimed at the murderous wolf, while their heartfelt sympathy is poured out for the devastated family of the slain sheep. With the passing of enough time, however, everything completely changes. Society often turns their sympathy toward the plight of the condemned inmate facing execution, while their contempt is aimed at the family of the slain sheep, because they are still crying out for justice.

I have worked with enough families of murder victims to know that the depth of their pain and suffering is tremendous. I have acquired many valuable nuggets of wisdom by listening to the different ways these families have learned to deal with their pain and loss. Many times, God used me to minister to them, but sometimes He used *them* to minister to *me*. God provided a particularly special blessing to me through one victim who allowed me to interview her and gave me permission to share some of her amazing story.

X Debbie's Story

Debbie Cuevas was a delightful and energetic sixteen-year-old girl who regularly made the school honor roll, served diligently on the student council, was a high school cheerleader, and was very active in her church youth group. She enjoyed the many blessings associated with living in a small town, including tranquil spring nights when she could go out with her boyfriend, Mark. One Friday night, after taking in a movie and a pizza, Debbie and Mark ordered milkshakes from the town's only drive-in and drove just a couple of blocks to the riverfront to enjoy them. Parked just a stone's throw from a dockside restaurant to the left and the tavern by the bridge to the right, they were surrounded by the familiar sights and sounds of the local nightlife. There was enough solitude, however, to roll down their windows and sip their shakes between giggles and small talk as their date was winding down to a close. Peering through the moss-laden branches of the giant oak trees, they watched the moonlight glistening off the water. It was a beautiful river. It was a wonderful little town. Both of them had grown up there. It was home—a safe, secure, quiet place.

Because they were nearing the end of their date, they didn't really mind when the white truck pulled up next to them in the parking lot, interrupting some of the serenity. But suddenly, two men jumped out and strong-armed their way into Mark's '78 T-bird at gunpoint. The gunmen told the young couple that they were only after their car and their money. When told they would be killed if they did not cooperate, Debbie and Mark decided not to resist.

The men drove them outside of town to a remote area. When they finally stopped the car, the men hit Mark over the head with a sawed-off shotgun and dumped his body into the trunk of the car. The ordeal that followed was an unspeakable nightmare of terror that would shatter Debbie's perfect little world and completely tear her life apart. She was raped repeatedly and abused until she felt detached from reality. When Mark was finally let out of the trunk, the two men tied him up, tortured him, and shot him in the back of the head. These abductors had raped and murdered another young girl only days earlier, and her body was in those same woods, just a short distance away from where Debbie was now being abused. As Debbie listened to the two men discuss the manner in which they were now going to kill her, an absolute miracle happened that defies human understanding. The men suddenly changed their minds and decided to release Debbie and let her live.

Strange and rare is the occasion when a victim of the person being executed for capital murder is still alive and able to share the details of that victimization. Yet Debbie, who was horribly victimized, did live to see the day when her assailant would be executed for another capital murder. Usually, the fragmented lives of the victims' families are all that remain in the wake of a capital murder. The plight of these families attempting to recover and emotionally survive the nightmare is sad, but Debbie Cuevas, now Debbie Morris, gives us a helpful and insightful perspective of a Christian victim's struggle with the assault and the execution.

I was not personally involved in Debbie's story, as one of the perpetrators of the horrible crimes against her was executed for a different crime in the state of Louisiana. However, after learning Debbie's story, I realized that not only was her amazing testimony a combination of all of the varied attitudes of victims' families I have observed over the years, but it also culminates in the best possible state of restoration and blessedness.

Debbie had become a Christian only two years before her ordeal. She imagined that her new relationship with Christ meant immunity from problems. Therefore, when she fell victim to such horrible atrocities, her perception of God was shattered. She felt an intense anger toward God for letting all of that happen to her. It seemed her trust in Him had been trampled. Debbie couldn't understand why the God she loved had let her down and did not protect her. Debbie had physically survived the assault, but she was emotionally destroyed. She became progressively consumed with anger toward her abductors, her family, and God. Her failed struggle to resume a normal life only made her angrier inside. She fell into a state of depression, which led to a drinking problem. Her life spun out of control.

In the final weeks preceding the execution of her assailant, Debbie experienced severe anxiety. She was emotionally tortured by the awareness of how much anger and hate she harbored inside. The haunting fear of the dark that she had developed was now replaced by the fear of her own anger. The stronghold of anger had paralyzed her soul and promised to keep her shackled to her pain long after the execution of her abductor. She realized that the death of the man who violated her would never heal her wounds and scars. Only after years of exhausting all other means and efforts to restore her life did she face the fact that the God she angrily ran away from was her only real hope for healing and restoration.

On the night of the execution, Debbie turned to God in prayer. When she forgave her assailant before God and surrendered her anger and hate, she felt a definite sense of peace and freedom. Her road to recovery had taken its biggest and most important step. Her struggle to become whole again was blessed with success only when she learned to forgive. Debbie accepted the fact that she, too, was a sinner and that God loved and valued a lost sheep like her assailant as much as He loved her.

Insights from Debbie help us to begin to comprehend the emotional and spiritual struggles of all of those who are in some way hurt and victimized by a condemned inmate. Debbie later married and is now a gifted speaker, sharing her message of forgiveness across the country.

[X] Execution Night Emotions

On some execution nights, the forgiving attitudes of the victims' families were far greater than my own, and I didn't even know the victims. Every execution worked on my emotions, but some of the strongest emotional peaks came from being with the families and friends of murder victims. My heart ached for those lives that were almost as destroyed as the actual murder victims'. So many of them seemed hopelessly enslaved to the torturous memories of what had happened to their loved ones.

The attitudes of the victim's family were new and different every time. We always studied the circumstances of the crime and the witnesses' relation to the victim before meeting them to give us a heads up on the people we were dealing with. Some nights we dealt with the parents of a murdered child; other nights it was the children of murdered parents. Occasionally we would have a person who had lost a spouse to capital murder. More than once the victim's family and the condemned inmate's family were one and the same—when someone had murdered his or her own child, parent, sibling, or spouse.

Every possible emotion was displayed in the witness rooms. Some witnesses were full of intense anger, vengeance, and hate; others were weeping and full of pain; and still others were bland, silent, and seemingly emotionless. Once in a while I saw witnesses who were sympathetic toward and had compassion for the condemned inmate who murdered their family member. Of all the different types, characters, and attitudes I saw, however, one thing was always the same. It was always obvious that these people were reliving the crime and the trial process all over again in their hearts and minds. Some of the executions carried out were for crimes committed over twenty years earlier, and still the family relived it anew on that day. The average duration from crime to execution is approximately ten years. The passing of time may heal a broken heart, but these poor people have to start that time all over by facing the murderer once again.

It appeared as though whatever wounds had been healed over were cut wide-open again by witnessing the execution. I would imagine that dealing with a loved one's murder is more devastating than dealing with any other form of family death. The feelings of loss and emptiness that arise with the sudden or unexpected death of a loved one are unimaginable; but adding the knowledge that your loved one was terrorized, abused, and brutally murdered would surely tear an even bigger jagged and gaping hole in your heart.

Many movies and books portray graphic and sickening scenes of violence, but they are only scratching the surface of what actually goes on out there in the real world. Satan tried hard to use my encounters with victims' families to provoke me to inappropriate levels of anger and even outright hatred toward the condemned inmate. One night I would be dealing with a family whose eighty-three-year-old grandmother was raped and murdered; then the next night I was dealing with the family of a little seven-year-old girl who was abducted and raped, then murdered.

I was a firsthand witness to the wreck that was made of these families' lives. Sometimes their anxiety and emotions would continue to escalate, only to hear at the last minute that a stay of execution had been granted. This creates one of the strangest dichotomies I have ever witnessed. The family of the condemned celebrates and rejoices in one room while the family of the victim is crushed and deflated in the other, their long awaited hope and desire for closure and peace annihilated. The family of the victim feels slapped in the face and victimized again. In all likelihood, they will return to undergo the same emotional roller-coaster ride and relive the pain yet one more time. I have no idea how much closure and peace, if any, families of victims get from witnessing executions, and I would assume they don't know for certain what they will gain when they arrive at the death chamber either. But some have shared that they were desperate for anything to provide them some escape from their nightmares of the perpetrator escaping or getting paroled and coming after them as well.

☒ The Peace of God

There was a noticeable difference in the countenance of families that possessed a strong faith in Jesus. I could always see that they had been blessed with peace by the one and only true source. Thanks to God's healing and comforting hand, these were the only witnesses who were not emotional basket cases of anxiety and confusion. The pain and sadness of reliving that horrible time in their lives was always visibly there, but one could tell that their loss and emptiness had been soothed by a special cover of God's grace. Although the forces of evil brought them great suffering and pain, their steadfast faith in God was rewarded as He lifted them up and held them close. One family proclaimed that the victory cry of the faithful in Micah 7:8 was theirs: "Rejoice not over me, O my enemy; when I fall, I shall rise; when I sit in darkness, the LORD will be a light to me."

I know I've never been in these people's shoes and can't fully understand how they feel; nevertheless, it is an even sadder and more difficult plight for families whose words and actions plainly show they are going through their suffering during the execution process without Jesus. They have found no peace whatsoever. Rather, they are deeply tormented by the anger, hate, and vengeance that has entangled and imprisoned their hearts and lives. Their anger is completely understandable. Going through the nightmare of such a tragic loss would make anyone angry at the wolf who caused it all. But letting the sun go down on that anger night after night, year after year, without asking for God's help would make the nightmare even worse.

One poor mother, whose young daughter was murdered, was outraged and furious at Chaplain Jim Brazzil because he had been praying for the condemned inmate's salvation. She told Jim, "Don't you dare pray for that man to end up in the same heaven as my daughter whom he murdered!" My heart went out to this mother because the depth of her pain was as obvious as the intensity of her anger.

Of all the times my heart struggled, this mother's words may have caused the worst tug-of-war of them all. I had never thought about a murderer being reunited with his victim in heaven. As I prayed for her, I also prayed for the condition of my own heart as I contemplated this new dilemma. Then God helped me consider that her heart was basically the same as that of the prophet Jonah. When God called Jonah to reach out to the lost souls at Nineveh, he refused because they were murderous wolves and he hated them. Jonah wanted the people of Nineveh to die and go straight to hell for all of the bloody violence and murder they committed against his people.

God showed me in the Book of Jonah that He cares about human wolves and reaches out in love even to the most wretched and despicable murderer. God also warned me that righteous anger can turn into unrighteous hate that can lead my heart astray. Jonah hated the people of Nineveh more than he loved God. I have seen many families of victims in this same condition. There was nothing left for me to do in such situations but pray for those families to be healed, comforted, and enabled to escape their torment through the peace of Christ. Admittedly, I had to pray the same prayer for myself sometimes whenever Satan succeeded in tugging my heart too far in that same "Jonah" direction.

☒ Why Did God Let This Happen?

There are many heartrending moments that occur during executions. I often saw large numbers of police officers show up at the Walls Unit from the city or department who lost a fellow officer at the hand of the man we were executing. It was quite emotional to see the display of respect, loyalty, and support of these officers who obviously bonded in a strong, serious relationship and were feeling the sting of having one of their own gunned down in the line of duty. It continuously left a big lump in my throat to see a gathering of big, tough, brawny guys in uniform crying and hugging one another for encouragement. I have always admired and appreciated the men and women from all of the different branches of law enforcement, but witnessing this sad and painful part of their lives gave me an immeasurable level of respect for what they do.

I praise God for raising up some among us who love their fellow man enough to answer the call to become professional crime fighters. They exemplify what Christ showed and explained to us in John 15:13: "Greater love has no one than this, that someone lay down his life for his friends." All crime fighters (and their families) accept and live with the reality that on any given night, they could easily become one of the many who lay down their lives to serve and protect others.

I suppose the worst thing victims' families have to endure, at times, is when the condemned inmate is giving his last words and he turns his head to face the family, taunts them, and abuses them with horrible comments about their loved one whom he violated and murdered. On some such occasions, we have been forced to execute men in midsentence, because they were obviously committed to using their last words for violating and attacking the family of the victim as long as they had breath to do so.

Many victims' families blame themselves for not having been able to prevent the crime, or for not protecting their loved one. They apparently feel that witnessing the execution is their only means of making up for not being there when the victim needed them. The families of victims are often tormented by questions they can't stop asking and haven't received any answers for. Christian and non-Christian alike often ask:

Why did God let this happen?
Where was God when my loved one was being murdered?
If she had to die, why did she have to suffer like that?
Will my heart ever stop hurting?
Will I ever recover and live happily again?

I watched so many hurting people wrestle with those thoughts that I found myself constantly searching God's Word for a deeper understanding of His will and purpose when innocent people suffer so terribly. I found that in all of God's dealing with mankind, He has never stopped trying to draw all of us closer to Himself for a deeper and eternal relationship. Every event in our lives, including suffering, has the distinct purpose of creating an opportunity for us to draw one more step closer to Him.

Some victims' families mentioned that they had a big problem with the thought of God using their suffering and pain for His purposes. I had to regularly remind myself that Jesus never told us life would be easy. As a matter of fact, He promised us that a life of following Him would be more difficult and full of trouble (Matthew 10:16–38). But He also promised that He would be with us always (Matthew 28:20). I asked the Lord to never allow me to forget that He did not say "if" we have trouble He would be with us, but rather the Lord specifically said "when." He makes it clear that we will indeed have trouble as long as we are in this temporary earthly life (Isaiah 43:2).

☒ Tested by Fire

God gave me another heart-shaping lesson through the family of a certain police officer, whose name will remain anonymous. The family of this officer became one of the biggest blessings God has ever given to my wife and me. Our relationship began in the darkest moment of their lives. The officer was diligently patrolling to provide extra protection to residents of a troubled neighborhood when he was killed in the line of duty. His assailant was eventually convicted of capital murder and sentenced to death. The officer's heroism helped restore the safety and stability of that neighborhood, but it was at the cost of the emotional stability of his family, as his wife lost her husband and his children lost their father. Only a couple of weeks after their loss, one of their friends brought them to the small-group Bible study that met in our home. As God arranged it, my wife, Jill, and I wrapped our hearts around this family and walked with them through the hell on earth that they endured for the months and years following the murder.

The wife of the slain officer was in complete shock and emotionally numb from the impact of the sudden and unexpected loss of her best friend and life mate. As the months rolled by after the crime, she sank into total despair and depression. The reality of the fact that her husband would never hold her or share anything with her ever again settled in like a thick, suffocating fog that engulfed her very soul. The awareness of what her husband physically endured while he was dying from the gunshot wounds tormented her to the point of an unquenchable agony of grief. She lost all desire to remain living. The future she faced promised nothing but deeper darkness and a growing emptiness.

The officer's children were suddenly left without their daddy. Their once promising future was now shaken and empty, much like their mother's. The children were understandably angry and bewildered at the thought of having to go through life without their dad as their trusted confidant and anchor. God allowed and enabled Jill and me to come alongside them and be one of His instruments to hold their hands and their hearts.

Within the first year after the officer's death, God powerfully answered our prayers as we began to witness this family's plight of despair and defeat take an amazing turn. In the midst of their indescribably deep pain and suffering, they firmly resolved to place their hope and trust in the mercy of God. They took a deep dive into complete and total dependence on the Lord for the strength to face each day. The pain and suffering did not miraculously disappear, but God honored their faith and drew them closer and closer to Himself daily. That family became the most amazing validation of God's Word that all things do indeed work together for those who love Him and are called according to His purpose (Romans 8:28). Their pain was real and ever present, but their trust in God was even more real. Not only did they survive the tragedy, but they also developed a level of faith and a deep personal relationship with their Lord that was stronger than a mighty oak and bore an astounding outpouring of the fruit of the Spirit through their lives.

God humbled me to see how incredibly greater this family's level of faith was beyond my own. Their faith walk through the valley of the shadow of death taught me that someone's darkest season of trouble will probably become the greatest defining moment in that person's life. It can be a crucial fork in the road, where a choice of direction will determine an entire future. This family decided to lean on Jesus while they were falling. They showed me that when wounded sheep come to the point of trusting the Shepherd in the middle of the most painful crisis of their lives, then today's struggles will be tomorrow's blessings. We human beings instinctively walk by sight rather than by faith, focusing on the pain of the moment. Crushing defeats make us feel as if God has let us down. Even the apostles felt that way when they asked Jesus, "Do You not care?" (Mark 4:38). Peter was one of the frightened, suffering apostles who asked Jesus that question, but later in his life he recorded this Spirit-led knowledge for us:

In this you rejoice, though now for a little while, if necessary, you have been grieved by various trials, so that the tested genuineness of your faith—more precious than gold that perishes though it is tested by fire—may be found to result in praise and glory and honor at the revelation of Jesus Christ. (1 Peter 1:6–7)

I learned that being tested by fire is never fun, but God's purpose for us is greater than any problem we will ever face. We have comforting counsel from Jesus in Matthew 5:3: "Blessed are the poor in spirit." A broken and contrite spirit does not think that it is too good to suffer. Hearts that are truly humble do not feel wronged by God when they are brought low by a season of hardship or loss; rather, they are always reaching out for His grace. They know, as Job did, that the Lord gives and the Lord takes away (Job 1:21). Those who totally depend on God's grace to sustain them in times of pain and trial are declared "blessed." Jesus gives the comforting promise of the kingdom of heaven to those who are humbly poor in spirit. There is no easy way to learn this life lesson. The pathway to this form of blessedness is lined with many tears, but also with God's grace.

On this side of heaven I will never understand all of God's will during the most difficult times of my life, but He always shows me enough of His grace to comfort and bless me in the moment. The Good Shepherd allowed me to discover a lot about what really matters to Him concerning the broken hearts of His sheep who have been ravaged by murderous wolves. The Lord used my interactions with the families of the victims to help me learn many lessons about forgiveness and trusting Him.

My heart still struggles to make sense of the far-reaching devastation caused by senseless acts of murder. However, the lack of understanding that used to pull my heart in conflicting directions became one of the most valuable forces in shaping me. When I found myself consistently trusting God in the midst of troubling situations that made no sense, I felt my faith growing. Those moments when my understanding came to an end became the point where my faith began. Each time I accepted the fact that I did not need to understand everything, the Holy Spirit would empower me with greater discernment than I possessed on my own.

Not all families of victims were forgiving and trusting in the Lord, but God used those who were to shape me toward having a more godly heart for the families of the condemned.

CHAPTER 8

Shaped by Families of the Condemned

The last thing on any young parents' minds as they celebrate the birth of their new child is that some day that little baby will grow up to become a murderer. When a young family dreams about all the things their child will eventually achieve, those dreams never include him or her being sent to death row. Every year, however, thousands of heartbroken American families must deal with the harsh reality that one of their own children has chosen to live by the sword of violence and has committed murder. No one ever wants their child to be known by society as a feared and dangerous wolf, but families find themselves in that unfortunate position every day.

Quite often, while dealing with the families of the condemned, I found them to be strong Christians who tried to raise their child according to biblical principles, but their efforts were not heeded. God blessed my heart by allowing me to observe some families of condemned inmates display faithful, stubborn love for their troubled child regardless of what he had done. What a parallel to the love God has for all of us occasionally wayward sheep!

The families who remained loyally supportive despite their loved one's crime or death sentence were a serious inspiration to me. Most families of condemned inmates were withdrawn and not very interested in conversing with me. Occasionally, however, some felt the need to talk about what was on their minds and shared their deepest feelings. I never asked for that level of communication, but I was always willing to listen and sincerely empathize with what spilled out of their broken hearts.

☒ The Prodigal Son

One mother, Gloria, told me that she had read the story of the prodigal son countless times. She said she found her life's calling in that story. As she explained her stubborn love for her son on the evening we executed him, Jesus' parable of the prodigal son in Luke 15:11–20 came alive in front of me.

Jesus explained that the father of the prodigal agreed to let his son stray from the family for a life of reckless living. Despite the young man's arrogant disobedience and rebellious betrayal, his father never stopped looking and hoping for his return. This meant that the father of the disrespectful rebel trusted God through the worst of consequences his son had to face. The father hurt as much as his prodigal son hurt, but allowed him to leave, crash, and learn the hard way.

Gloria told me that in this parable, Jesus was describing our heavenly Father's loving relationship with her son as an example for her to follow. She explained how, in the early years of his rebelliousness, she did not let her son go into God's hands. Instead, she bailed him out, rescued him with attorneys, and made sure that he never hit the bottom of the pig pen. Her son knew she would always be there despite each increasingly serious crime and arrest.

Only after her son fell into deeper trouble than she and her attorneys could resolve did she realize that she had been a part of the problem by enabling him to keep going and never feel the consequences of his actions. Gloria said that she covered up for him with family, school, and the church until he landed in the pig pen by committing capital murder.

Only then did Gloria follow the counsel of the Lord in the story of the prodigal son. She let go and let God be in control of his life. Her son could not physically return home, but he did return to God with his heart. Only then did she escape the bondage of worry and no longer live in fear and grief. When she gave her son to God in trust, she was finally able to be the parent she knew she should be.

She was still there for her son. She still faithfully loved him. But she did what the father of the prodigal did—she let him go and trusted God. Whatever happened to him, she knew that God was in control. She was at peace. I truly admired and appreciated that mother's faith as well as the faith of other families who followed the example of that parable by remaining stubbornly loyal and faithful to their family member on death row.

[X] Where Did I Go Wrong?

Living through the countdown to execution day is tough and painful for the families of the condemned inmates. They never want the execution date to arrive. When it does, they dread their role as witnesses—wishing somehow they had never been thrust into this world of capital punishment. For these families, everything in life is seen from a different perspective from the time the crime was committed. The family of the condemned inmate is stunned when their child is arrested, devastated when the jury returns from the deliberation with the verdict of guilty, and crushed when the sentence of death is announced. From that day on, the family of the condemned wrestles with emotional turmoil and is helplessly stuck in an awkward and painful position.

Families of condemned inmates have told me that it is a long and extremely difficult path to follow in trying to deal with a family member on death row. Their attempts to grieve and sort everything out in their hearts and minds is constantly interrupted by bombarding thoughts of disbelief, anger, and self-blame. Many parents can't stop asking themselves the same tormenting questions: "Where did I go wrong in raising him?" "What could I have done differently?" From what I see, it appears that a great many of these poor parents are unable to stop a downward emotional spiral into deeper depression and despair. One of the most graphic illustrations of such despondency is found in the Bible, where David cries out to God in Psalm 6:2–7a:

> *Be gracious to me, O LORD, for I am languishing;*
> *heal me, O LORD, for my bones are troubled. My*
> *soul also is greatly troubled. But You, O LORD — how*
> *long? Turn, O LORD, deliver my life; save me for the*
> *sake of Your steadfast love. For in death there is no*
> *remembrance of You; in Sheol who will give You*
> *praise? I am weary with my moaning; every night I*
> *flood my bed with tears; I drench my couch with my*
> *weeping. My eye wastes away because of grief.*

It was sad for me to witness so many people going through such an affliction of grief, all because a family member chose to live by the sword of violence. Thousands of Americans are enveloped in that pain right now, having to cope with a loved one in prison or on death row.

One mother described her feelings as being buried under such a heavy mountain of sorrow and heartbreak that her energy and strength to carry on with daily life had been completely drained. She told me that even if she could find the strength to lift up her head and resume a normal life, she wouldn't know how to begin putting the pieces back together again. She said that she could not bring herself to watch television or movies any longer, because the story line of most movies involves a hated and dangerous villain as the antagonist who needs to be defeated and destroyed. She explained that Satan causes her to think of her son to be the hated villain, which buries her under unspeakable grief. This mother stated that her friends, family, and even her pastor always act like they are walking on eggshells around her in fear that they will accidentally step on her fragile emotions and send her reeling back into depression. She hates that they have to do that but is thankful that they do, because she fears they are right.

Fortunately, not all of the loved ones of condemned inmates remain in this bondage of defeat and despondency. I was able to hear some of them describe how they once felt that same crushing weight of hopelessness but had been liberated from those shackles by Christ. I marveled at the mercy and grace of God in their deliverance, because I had learned so much about the depth of the emotional dungeon from which they were miraculously rescued.

My appreciation for the rescuing power of the Lord increased each time I would see a once broken and defeated family member of a condemned inmate testify that Jesus was the one and only source of deliverance from those seemingly insurmountable afflictions.

Jesus promised us:

Come to Me, all who labor and are heavy laden, and I will give you rest. Take My yoke upon you, and learn from Me, for I am gentle and lowly in heart, and you will find rest for your souls. For My yoke is easy, and My burden is light. (Matthew 11:28–30)

I learned that there is great peace in close fellowship with God, regardless of the circumstances the families of the condemned are enduring. Even in the midst of suffering that they didn't understand, they received comfort and peace every time they cried out to God and leaned on Him.

☒ A Mother's Love

In the years that follow sentencing, a parent, spouse, child, or sibling will usually write and visit the inmate as often as possible. The most common relative to faithfully visit and write is the mother. The mother is also the most common witness from the inmate's family on execution night. It used to amaze me how a mother would want to witness the execution of her child. After participating in enough executions, however, I realized that if it were my son, I would be there to show him support and hopefully be of some comfort to him. I suppose a mother would not want her child to go through that alone, and if just standing there letting him know he is loved is all she can do for her son, I understand why she would do that for him.

I am convinced that the presence of the inmate's mother causes him to be on his best behavior for her sake, so from a security perspective, I appreciated mothers being there. Most of the time, mothers are a huge asset to security in the prison system. I often saw inmates with zero fear or concern for any disciplinary control measures we might use, yet many of those same inmates feared accountability to "Mom." Sometimes the greatest deterrent penalty I could threaten to use against a dangerous and disruptive inmate was to "tell their mom." Some of the penalties I gave out in inmate disciplinary court restricted or suspended the ability to receive visits. Many inmates would rather take any other severe penalty than not to be able to see their moms on weekends. I once was holding court on the biggest, meanest-looking brute of an inmate when, in the middle of the hearing, he broke down and cried like a baby, begging me to not take away his time with his mom.

One of the instruments most used by God to bless us with His peace through the toughest times of our life journey is our mother. In the midst of an execution for the worst of crimes, nothing will more effectively distract you from dwelling on the details of the murderous event than to witness the love between the criminal and his mother. It can catch you off guard. It's like pausing to be brought down to another reality by tenderness in the midst of travail.

I wish all condemned inmates had this type of loving family support in the final moments of their lives, but that is not the case. Many inmates have no immediate family witnesses on their execution night, because their families did not support them and remain faithful to them after their crime. As sad as this situation is, however, God always offers a light of His love to those who have been abandoned on this earth. For those who accept His offer, He gives them an "extended family" to be an instrument of His love as a comforting light in their darkest hour. God has taught me volumes about His love through those who have answered the call to be an extended family to a lost and abandoned human wolf on death row.

X   Loving the Unlovable

On one particularly quiet Texas night, Interstate 45 was slick and icy with freezing rain still falling, making driving conditions more dangerous by the moment. Daybreak was still a good six hours away, and the dark, frozen highway was almost completely deserted except for an occasional cautiously moving eighteen-wheeler and one little maroon Chevrolet Corsica, stubbornly defying the hazardous conditions. The little car was driven by a wide-awake and intently focused Kathryn Cox. Her destination of death row near Huntsville, Texas, was at least four more hours of hard driving ahead through the night. She would always be sure to arrive at the prison unit well on time to begin her full day of visiting with and ministering to the inmates on death row.

Ms. Cox made this trip and worked with death row inmates virtually every week for twenty-five years. She was actually Major Cox with the Salvation Army. This energetic, hard-working soldier of God began working with the Salvation Army in 1933! Over seventy years later, Major Cox had not slowed down one bit in her persistent and tenacious outreach to teach, counsel, and pray with death row inmates. For many condemned inmates, Kathryn is the only family they have. Many of the residents on death row get loyal, regular visits from their families, but most do not. Some of the families of these inmates have no desire to visit them, and some of these inmates want no part of their families either.

Some inmates are on death row for a crime that mirrors the way they themselves were reared and treated as children. Many a heinous crime is the ultimate result of a character molded and warped by family members who molested and despicably abused them throughout their childhood. For some inmates, the existence or description of a loving Father in heaven or a caring church family are images that they can in no way comprehend. When a minister tries to sow the seed of God's Word to someone like this, it is usually seed that falls on infertile ground. These men and women are so deep in darkness that numerous attempts from many different ministries to share the Good News with them is no more effective than seed sown on the path that is immediately snatched away by the enemy (Mark 4:14–15).

It amazes me how some people have answered the call to keep sowing good seed onto an infertile path and to continuously persist in showing concern for the "least of these" until they eventually become fertile ground. Kathryn Cox regularly visited with some of these inmates for decades before peeling off enough layers of hate and bitterness to help an inmate truly listen to the Gospel and be enabled to receive the grace of God. Kathryn routinely endured years of being rudely disrespected and horribly blasted with obscenities and vulgarities. The men she faithfully worked with often mistreated, cursed, and threatened her for years before finally realizing that nothing they did could stop this lady and her God from loving them. I believe that many an executed inmate is in heaven today because of the relentless efforts of this one Christian soldier who stubbornly loved unlovable wolves until God worked the miracle of giving them ears to hear, enabling them to become His sheep.

Love for human wolves certainly did not come naturally to me, but when I drew close enough to God, I heard His voice in His Word calling me to love them. Unconditional love for the completely unlovable is the greatest representation of the true family of God on earth. Kathryn Cox was that true godly family in many different ways. She was instrumental in helping reconcile and reunite estranged families with death row inmates. She stood by and supported dozens of inmates at the hour of their death by witnessing their execution at an inmate's request, and she attended hundreds of funerals for them.

Many inmates are blessed with families who still love and care for them, but for all those who are not, God is faithful to provide an "extended family" to reach out to them. Thank God there are many ministers who serve the Lord in this way. Our Father is continuously reaching out to bless both sheep and wolves alike through the instruments of His faithful servants. For countless death row inmates, their most valuable blessing in life was the love of God extended through the instrument of Major Kathryn Cox.

I learned so much about having a servant's heart from Kathryn. I was drawn to her by the obvious presence of Christ in her life. She displayed an almost inconceivable degree of love for prodigals that I did not yet have. I was able to spend a lot of time with her when she came to Huntsville, and she became a very good friend. I was so impressed by her heart of ministry that I drove to Dallas one time just to learn more about her ministry with the Salvation Army. God certainly molded my heart into a greater capacity to know the Truth and serve Him by exposing me to the witness of this dear sister.

☒ Visitation Weekends

Another way I learned about an inmate's definite need for love and acceptance from the Body of Christ was by working on visitation weekends. I supervised visitation once a month for eighteen years, during which time I met and spoke with thousands of inmates' families. I've seen some mothers have up to five different children in prison and travel from unit to unit visiting them on weekends. A lot of inmates' families are extremely impoverished, but many also come from the middle and upper-middle class. After a few minutes of conversing with an inmate's parents, siblings, or spouse, I would walk away from that discussion either wondering how the inmate could come from such a great, loving family and make such stupid choices and decisions, or I'd walk away understanding quickly and easily how someone raised in such a family could end up in prison or on death row.

Some parents are as rough, coarse, and mean as any inmate we've ever had. Many parents are also ex-convicts, and some spouses are ex-convicts as well. When I saw what some of these inmates had for parents, I felt sorry for them; I imagined that life in prison might actually be easier than growing up in a family environment of constant crudeness and cruelty of all types.

Many times I've narrowly avoided serious violent confrontations with an inmate's family. On one occasion, an inmate's spouse ended an angry verbal assault on me by pointing at me and telling the small child holding her hand, "Get a good look at that uniform, son. Bad men like him are why your daddy has to be in prison and can't come home to be with us!" The poor little kid was being trained to follow his daddy's footsteps into prison.

One time, an inmate's wife argued furiously with me that her husband should not be in prison because, as she put it, "Our ten-year-old daughter is a tramp and never should have snitched on him because she was making him have sex with her all those years anyway." This was by far the saddest example I witnessed of a horribly dysfunctional and sick family. Learning what kinds of families exist out there was a cold, ugly, rude awakening for me as to how and why some children can grow up to become criminals. No, this does not excuse their criminal offenses, but it does help us to have mercy and accept them as family in the Body of Christ.

I knew there were many inmates who received no mail, no visits, and no phone calls, nor did they have family who would claim them. One of the most sobering and depressing experiences I saw time and again was when the family of executed death row inmates completely disowned them and even refused to claim their bodies. Those inmates were always buried the very next morning in the prison cemetery, which is mostly for unwanted inmates or families who choose to forgo a free-world burial. I have attended many inmates' funerals with absolutely no one present aside from the chaplain and myself. I can't think of a more chilling example of the end result of a life lived for self—no one to care that you ever lived, no one to care that you're gone.

The moments I recall of standing out in the middle of the inmate cemetery beside those caskets are indeed gloomy and somber memories. Some free-world funerals are filled with rejoicing and celebration of a life God used to bless others. Some free-world funerals are filled with mourning. But many death row funerals are full of only silence and emptiness. At that time of the morning, there is nothing but stillness. There is often not even so much as a breeze blowing.

This is the State of Texas' inmate cemetery in Huntsville, where many death row inmates are buried the morning after their execution.

Sometimes the silence can be deafening. Sometimes it can be an opportunity for a profoundly deep encounter with the truth. I can recall standing there in the prison cemetery thinking that as blunt and as sad as the moment is, it is still only the beginning of the wages of sin for some of them.

If only I had the ability to remember the reality of such a scene every time I am tempted to withhold love and forgiveness for a human wolf. If I could, I would be much more likely to fulfill the Great Commandment (Matthew 22:36–39). I would be more like the faithful families of the condemned inmates who stubbornly loved their prodigal son despite how deeply he had broken their heart.

I will be forever thankful for the lessons I learned from the families and extended families of condemned inmates. Their perseverance in serving God by loving wolves who often don't even want their love is a priceless example of loving as God loves. These people who literally submit themselves to trials and sufferings in order to love someone are clear proof of the fruit of the Spirit in their life. They exemplify picking up the cross and following Jesus; knowing and accepting the cost of loving like Jesus loves; fighting the good fight with the theology of the cross; and trusting that God's promise in James 1:12 is true: "Blessed is the man who remains steadfast under trial."

I would still need to persevere through many more years of trials in the valley of the shadow of death row. My fights with human wolves were far from being over. My methods of fighting, however, were becoming more of the "good fight" that God desires.

CHAPTER 9

Shaped by Fighting the Good Fight

One of the major causes of fights between inmates is their fear of the hundreds of human wolves they constantly have to live with. Out of fear of being victimized, they will often fight to prove the point that they can be as much of a wolf as anyone else. This survival of the fittest mind-set can spawn from inappropriate and unhealthy fears and spiral downhill from there. What starts as primarily defensive motives often develops into offensive motives that become savagely aggressive inside the penitentiary.

The survival of the fittest mind-set usually starts as a youth in the schoolyard. It then continues to spread into neighborhood gangs. This leads to county jail prisoner associations. It finally reaches full-blown bloody chaos in the state penitentiary. Inappropriate fear can inadvertently make a deadly wolf out of a once peaceful sheep. This form of wolf training happens in every culture and in every community.

The vast majority of our inmate population in Texas comes from the three major metropolitan areas of Houston, Dallas, and San Antonio. Counties containing smaller cities and towns send inmates to the penitentiary also, but they send them in squad cars, while the "Big Three" send them by the busloads. I figured that the citizens living in and around a prison town like Huntsville, Texas, would have seen and heard enough about the horrors of penitentiary life to have made them extra conscientious about their personal behavior so as to avoid ever becoming incarcerated, but that was not the case. Many of our local citizens became inmates every year. Murders and capital murders (the law differentiates these two terms) were committed in and around our town frequently, and our citizens worked their way onto death row more often than I would have ever dreamed. Accordingly, there was an unhealthy fear of wolves even in my own little town.

I learned that no area or neighborhood is immune to predator attacks, because human wolves can come from any town and can strike anyone, anywhere, at any time. What is the appropriate response? What is a healthy fear? What is fighting the good fight? All of God's sheep must take reasonable, healthy precautions to avoid falling prey to wolves. But what kind of precautions should we take? Buy guns? Put burglar bars on our windows? Keep big dogs in our yard? Don't go out after dark? The answers to these questions are maybe, sometimes, and it all depends.

My primary and first tactic of defense should be prayer and dependence on God as my fortress, my shield, and my deliverer (Psalm 18:1–3). Although the Lord gives many different aspects of guidance on what to do when wolves ravage His flock, the most important area of counsel is for His sheep to not go through life held hostage by a fear of wolves. Accordingly, Proverbs 29:25 tells us that fear of man is a snare, but whoever trusts in the Lord is kept safe. The Bible tells me that I should also make efforts to strive for peace as much as possible (Romans 12:18). But what about those times when peace is not possible? I am commanded in 1 Timothy 5:8 to provide for my family in all ways, and this includes protection. Taking reasonable self-defense precautions and actions to protect my family is a serious responsibility. I am to follow the example of the Good Shepherd, and one of a shepherd's primary responsibilities is to protect his sheep and safely guide them through the valley of the shadow of death with his rod and his staff.

☒ Ministering to Wolves

While studying the Bible for how to fight the good fight, God led me to carefully consider Ephesians 6:1–17. I had always thought that this passage of Scripture dealt with only spiritual battles. God helped me realize, however, that the most important victories in our physical battles are actually won on the spiritual battlefield. God helps us win a lot of physical battles, but He is far more concerned with the spiritual battles that accompany them.

To assure a victory in the spiritual realm, I needed to approach my physical enemies first and foremost with a heart of ministry. If my heart and mind were consumed with a love for God and a desire to please Him, then my first thoughts about wolves would be concern for their souls (Matthew 5:43–48). If my heart is filled with compassion and sincere concern for my enemies, I will not live in fear of them.

I totally believed God's counsel, but living by that counsel required that I figure out how to have a heart of ministry toward dangerous wolves who were totally committed to living by the sword of violence. We had some inmates who were sentenced to death because juries considered them too dangerous to remain living. While awaiting their execution date on death row, they continued their commitment to violence by assaulting or murdering fellow inmates or prison guards. Some continued this bent until their final breath.

I will never forget the execution day of one such inmate who tried with all his might to keep his promise to kill as many guards as possible before we executed him. When it was time to bring him to the death house, he fought the death row transport team so ferociously that they had to use tear gas to subdue him. By the time they delivered him to the death house to be placed in the holding cell, he was bound with handcuffs, leg irons, a belly chain, and a neck brace; yet he still resisted as much as possible.

When we locked him inside the death house holding cell, he actually managed to pick the locks of every mechanical restraint that bound him. Within a matter of minutes, this inmate was freely roaming his cell, grasping the shackles and chains that were now his weapons. He proudly swung his weapons in the most intimidating fashion and vowed to kill anyone who tried to enter his cell.

This inmate did not want a last meal. He had no interest in talking to either the chaplain or me. All he was focused on was the fight. He was determined to die the same way he had lived—by the sword of violence. How do you minister to a wolf whose only interest is to destroy you? I can recall standing in front of his cell praying for him and feeling compassion for this person who was apparently immune to compassion. I remember thinking that the false sense of security he felt with the weapons he brandished was probably reflective of how he'd lived his entire life, and this was where such thinking had ultimately brought him.

This inmate paced back and forth in his cell like a boxer in his corner of the ring, awaiting the sound of the bell that announced the start of the fight. None of us were alarmed or overly concerned about his threats, because we knew he wasn't going anywhere and couldn't hurt anybody. We let him keep his trophies and roam his cell freely for a few hours. As the clock ticked closer to 6:00 p.m., the tie-down team began to put on their flack jackets, riot helmets, and other body armor in preparation to extract him from his cell. The rest of the team was preparing the IV tubes, getting the injections ready, and gathering the witnesses for entrance into the prison. The inmate continued taunting us and talking to himself, getting psyched up and ready for the fight. Our tie-down team was ready also, and at 6:00 p.m., his cell door was flung open.

The five-member tie-down team rushed in amid swinging chains and shackles and engaged this death house resident head-on. The team quickly and skillfully subdued the inmate, extracting him from his cell, but not without heavy and constant resistance every step of the way. The fight continued down the hallway, into the death chamber, and up onto the table. Even though it was five against one, this inmate put up a serious fight until the last restraining belt was fastened securely around him and he was finally lying motionless on the death gurney. Under the thick padding of the riot gear, the tie-down team was drenched in sweat and exhausted, but they sustained no injuries and performed their duty textbook perfect. The rest of the team stepped up with the remainder of their duties, and the execution process was completed without the condemned inmate getting his wish to take some of us with him.

I went home from that execution with a renewed interest in finding the most complete understanding of the apostle Paul's numerous references to "fighting the good fight." Paul invested a lot of ministry efforts toward wolves who rejected his message and tried to kill him. Were most of his efforts to minister to these people wasted? Does fighting the good fight mean you win some and lose some?

I realized that Christians who are called to be soldiers, police officers, and prison guards must physically fight to protect the citizens they serve. All of us, however, should make sure that the first and most utilized weapon in our arsenal is the sword of the Spirit (the Word of God). It is the most powerful and effective weapon we can use. There are definitely times when crime control and protecting the sheep from predatory wolves calls for meeting the sword of violence with the sword of violence. Yet, in using the weapons of the world, we will win some battles and lose some. Fighting the good fight with the sword of the Spirit, however, always assures us of victory in the battles that matter the most to God. Acts of ministry from hearts seeking to please and serve God as directed by the counsel of His Word are never wasted, even when the wolves seem to be winning.

X Spiritual Hostages

I learned that in fighting the good fight God counsels all of His sheep to confront evil by taking a bold stand for the truth. God knew that if I did not confront evil every day of my life, I would tolerate and condone it to avoid the conflict. God used my experience with the violently fighting condemned inmate who rejected all ministry efforts to teach me a valuable lesson.

The inmate who was swinging his collection of chains and iron shackles while shouting murderous threats to us thought he had basically taken us all hostage. He imagined that our fear of the confrontation would prevent or delay us from doing our duty. If we would have allowed him to succeed in that effort, we would have indeed been held hostage by him. If I had considered his rejection of attempted ministry as a sign that I should not even bother to pray for him and show him compassion, I would have failed to fight the good fight and the enemy would have been holding me spiritually hostage.

Inmates occasionally take prison employees as hostages; therefore we receive regular training on how to react in such a situation. In some of these training sessions, we are shown videos of hostage situations where those taken hostage fell victim to Stockholm syndrome. This is a condition where the hostage eventually sympathizes with the captor to the point of embracing his or her cause. Repeated similar occurrences of this syndrome have led criminologists to realize that when hostages fears their captor enough, they will become like their captor in an attempt to survive.

Understanding Stockholm syndrome actually showed me how easy it is for any sheep to be held spiritually hostage. Whenever any of us are afraid to confront evil, our fear enables the wolf to continue to believe that the lie he is following is worthy of his continued trust. It also puts us in the dangerous position of believing the same thing. We can become a living illustration of Proverbs 29:25. Whenever I was tempted to fear wolves, I remembered that I was actually fighting a spiritual battle. Physical battles in prison were fierce and constant, but I learned to use the sword of the Spirit first. This ultimate weapon always helped me win a spiritual victory even in the darkest moments.

I recall one afternoon when I was passing by one of our more peaceful cellblocks. The dayroom at the entrance of the cellblock was crowded with inmates returning from the chow hall, waiting to be racked up into their cells (opening their cell doors and allowing them to enter). The noise level was a loud commotion of cell doors slamming and dozens of inmates talking and hollering. A small, thin inmate maintenance worker was replacing a broken window in the dayroom at the time. He was quietly working and trying to ignore the much larger inmate who was heckling and badgering him. The larger inmate was basically trying to "take him hostage" by bullying him into granting sexual favors.

The big inmate bent down to make his taunting a little more personal and intimidating, but the smaller inmate swung around, quick as a cat, and thrust a ten-inch screwdriver deep into the center of the big guy's chest. He then pulled it out again to be ready for another strike if necessary. The big guy didn't seem to feel any pain, and there was no external bleeding, but he knew he was in serious trouble. He ran out of the cellblock and sprinted past me toward the unit infirmary. I helped the inmate get into the emergency room, where the doctors and nurses took his shirt off and asked him to lie down on the examining table. But as soon as the inmate lay down on the table, he died. Both of the inmates in this skirmish depended on the wrong thing for survival. This was one more testimony that those who depend on the weapons of this world will win some and lose some until they finally lose it all.

☒ God Is in Control

Unfortunately, I had become quite used to violence and death because of how common this type of occurrence was in our system. Family and friends used to ask me regularly, "Aren't you afraid when you are in there?" At the beginning of my career, my response to fear was to become aggressively and brutally offensive, which led to no fear of anything, including God. As God helped me humble myself before Him and walk closer with Him, I died to self, which led to no

♡
✝

fear of human wolves, only a reverent fear of God. After countless pride-killing lessons helped me to grow totally dependent on Jesus, getting hurt or killed by an inmate or anyone else was never a concern of mine. This wasn't because of a profound degree of courage, but rather a mustard-seed degree of faith. My progressive growth through studying God's Word and drawing closer to Him over the years firmly formed my feelings about death and dying. I have never desired a long life; rather, I have just trusted in God's protection and tried to responsibly use each day as if it were my last. The Lord might very well allow some tragic accident or violent act to bring an early end to my life. If so, He has a reason and a purpose beyond my current understanding, and I accept that. Basically, I know that when God is ready for me to leave this life, I'm leaving, and nothing can stop that. In the same way, until God is ready to allow my life on this earth to end, nothing or no one can take me out. The moment or method of my death will not take God by surprise.

Every man's life is filled with the constant and desperate attempts of the enemy to devour us, physically or spiritually. But for those who love God and are called according to His purpose, what the enemy intends for evil, God will ultimately use for good, even our death. God is in complete and absolute control. If His will is to allow me to die right now, then I don't want to stay on this earth one second longer because His will is perfect and I trust Him. I trust that He will protect me until He's ready to call me home, and if that is sooner rather than later, then that is exactly what I want. I don't know what today and tomorrow will hold, but I do know the One who holds today and tomorrow, and He is all I need. I will not allow potential dangers to distract me from trusting in Him.

My faith that God is in total control helped me to be an effective employee for both God and the state. Maintaining law and order in a dark and hostile wolf pen was difficult, but God enabled me to perform my duties with the necessary authoritarian demeanor yet still remain compassionate, even in the midst of gross violence. I was fully trained to respond to life-threatening situations. I certainly reacted to threatening situations in the most effective way possible, but it was in confidence, not in fear. This state of mind that I was able to maintain was one of the ways God answered my prayers to help me be as wise as a serpent but as innocent as a dove. The Lord helped me have the wisdom to respect dangerous situations but the innocence of a sheep that trusts his Shepherd. When I remembered how many times God answered my prayers and saved me from harm, I was able to think of threatening situations the same way young David did when he stated: "The LORD who delivered me from the paw of the lion and from the paw of the bear will deliver me from the hand of this Philistine" (1 Samuel 17:37).

Even though I frequently see people react to pressure with worry or discouragement, I resolved long ago to meet pressure with prayer. David did not defeat Goliath with strength and skill, nor did he face the giant with any fear. He told the enemy to his face, "You come to me with a sword and with a spear and with a javelin, but I come to you in the name of the LORD of hosts" (1 Samuel 17:45). Every time I was faced with dangers and obstacles in prison, I professed, "He who is in [me] is greater than he who is in the world" (1 John 4:4). I spoke out loud to the enemy, "My God will supply every need of [mine] according to His riches in glory" (Philippians 4:19). The Lord has indeed rescued me many times and proven to me that I can do all things through Christ who gives me strength (Philippians 4:13).

I once heard a worker from a prison ministry crusade team testify that he had been a Green Beret for several tours in Vietnam. The guy was a martial arts expert. He was big and muscular, and he definitely looked like a person no one would ever want to cross. He revealed, however, that after leaving the military and becoming a civilian, he found himself living in constant fear. He always carried a loaded weapon and a survival knife everywhere he went, because he suspected everyone of being a dangerous enemy. He slept with a semiautomatic handgun under his pillow and would awaken at the slightest bump in the night. This tough, strong, fighting machine testified that he was preoccupied with fear for years until he heard the Gospel of Jesus Christ, received His grace, and began to follow the Lord. He finally realized that only Jesus could and did deliver him from fear, insecurity, and paranoia. He began reading the Word and found that in Matthew 10:28, Jesus tells us, "Do not fear those who kill the body but cannot kill the soul. Rather fear Him who can destroy both soul and body in hell." This man excitedly revealed that he is now blessed with complete peace because he trusts in God, not in his weapons or his own strength. I've seen many inmates and free-world people alike who were once trusting entirely on their own strength become similarly transformed to relaxed, peaceful new creations in Christ.

Fear is a debilitating emotion that can cripple our faith and our life. The Word tells us in Jeremiah 17:7: "Blessed is the man who trusts in the LORD." Jesus counsels us to exhibit that trust by taking up our cross and following Him (Matthew 16:24). Whenever I was blessed with the grace to have enough faith to accept my cross, only then was I fighting the good fight by trusting in God for my daily survival. Rather than using my human wisdom to find ways to avoid the cross or make it easier to carry, my demonstration of faith was: "I will carry my cross because I know He will carry me." During the most life-threatening times, I would consider His grace far more sustaining than any physical strength of my own. I eventually came to trust my Shepherd so much that I actually felt peace during trials because I realized that He loved me enough to prune me like a gardener. I found such peace under His protection that I became eager to see what fruit this season of pruning would eventually bring forth in my life.

It seemed to me that the more I became empowered to take a biblical stand to confront evil, the more frequent those confrontations became. Despite my most sincere efforts to show compassion and concern toward hostile inmates, some of them would stop at nothing less than a violent physical altercation. Many of those inmates would have certainly killed me if they had a better opportunity. Some of those opportunities became available to inmates who were eventually discharged and found me outside the prison in the free world.

☒ Whom Shall I Fear?

One day I left the Walls Unit on my lunch break to drive across town to a small restaurant. I was looking forward to an hour of peace and quiet more than I was looking for good food. After being served, I was attempting to relax and enjoy my meal when three middle-aged men walked up and sat down at the table across from me. None of them appeared to have any interest in eating. Their reason for being there quickly became apparent as they all stared at me with taunting grimaces on their faces. All of them began to laugh at me and talk about how I didn't look so tough and powerful now. I recognized one of them as an inmate we had recently paroled and released back into the free world. I also remembered that I once had to subdue that inmate in a confrontation in the prison. One of his buddies nodded in my direction and asked him, "Is he the one?" With a vengeful glare in his eye and fiendish cackle in his voice, he answered, "Yeah, he's the one." They continued to stare at me and began to discuss among themselves what they were about to do to me. I never said a word to them. I was emotionally preparing myself for a whirlwind fight of the most serious degree. As I quickly planned in my mind the defensive moves and counter assault I was about to launch, I simultaneously asked God to let His will be done with these men.

Suddenly, like the silence before the storm, the atmosphere in that little restaurant turned completely quiet. All three men stopped taunting me and stood up. At that moment, I knew it was on and I silently prayed: "Let your will be done, Father." To my surprise, however, their faces turned from hostile to fearful. Within a few seconds, they all quickly and quietly walked out of the restaurant. I was so focused on the men and my prayer that I did not notice one of my friends, Jesse Oates, had walked up behind me. He was a fellow prison employee who worked in my department. Jesse was about six feet three inches tall and 310 pounds of mostly solid muscle. He was going to join me for lunch and did not realize at that moment what had happened, but the angry wolf pack of would-be assailants melted in fear and slithered away when he walked up. In answer to my prayer, God rescued me from the jaws of the wolves and mercifully delivered the wolves from Jesse and a quick trip to jail.

When those men were about to assault me, I was not sure what the outcome would be, but I was sure that God was in control. Even though I was unaware that Jesse was walking up to join me, I knew that I would not be facing that battle alone. It gave me such peace to be able to know and follow biblical counsel such as Psalm 27:1, "The LORD is my light and my salvation, whom shall I fear?" Anyone relying solely on his or her own abilities for protection against danger and threatening problems will ultimately become stressed out, exhausted, and defeated. We were never meant to face challenges on our own. Ask Goliath. Ask most any death row inmate. It doesn't matter how tough or how smart you are. Many of the residents on death row are brilliant. Many of them were smarter and tougher than anyone or anything they had ever faced until they faced the steel bars of their cells.

Once an inmate finally realizes that he is not ten feet tall and bullet proof, he finds himself facing a fork in the road ahead of him. Far too often, he turns the wrong direction for help. Many inmates join prison gangs for assistance in surviving the dangers of prison life. However, the unforeseen pitfalls of pledging allegiance to any person or group that does not include Christ at the center will never stay unforeseen for very long. Putting our faith and trust in anything other than God will always leave us disappointed at the very least and often leads to complete disaster. Most prison gangs are racial and ethnic brotherhood groups that bond together to have power over other groups or individuals. Every aspect of this type of arrangement is destructive. If a gang is not planning or carrying out violent assaults against its opponents, it is committing them against its own members as internal discipline. The very thing in which some inmates place their hope for security and survival ends up costing far more than it was ever worth.

In one of our routine in-service training sessions for our guards, we showed a video tape of an actual gang murder in progress. This specific incident, caught on tape in its entirety, showed two fellow "brothers" of the same gang recreating together. Suddenly, one of the men pounced on the other with a homemade knife that he had concealed on his body. The assailant proceeded to carry out the execution of his "brother" gang member as ordered by the gang leaders. While most of the guards watching this video had their minds and senses focused on the bloody, barbaric violence unfolding before us, my mind was thinking that this unfortunate scene was actually an extremely predictable disclosure of the truth about misplaced hope and trust. Members of gangs usually have to learn that truth lesson the hard way. About the only thing Satan loves more than a self-reliant, godless person is an entire organization of such people. Both were established by Satan himself. Who else could ever build such a group of self-serving, yet codependent people? The key to survival for an inmate is the same for any free world person. Any form of security established upon a foundation other than the truth of Jesus Christ will fail.

X Founded on the Rock

If I am going to lean on a human for strength and support, it will be a prayer partner and brother in the Lord. Bonding with others for support when Christ is in fact the center of that union is indeed a powerful and helpful alliance (Ecclesiastes 4:12). Actually, there is no limit to the power of such an organization! Jesus assured us in Matthew 18:20 that "where two or three are gathered in My name, there am I among them." The Shepherd is with us in the sheepfold. There can be no greater sense of security than to know this. If we stay close to the Good Shepherd, there is no need to fear because we are in the safety of the Truth. Anyone grounded in the Truth will stand securely and not be swept away by lies. I was enabled to grow close enough to the Lord to firmly believe these words He spoke:

Everyone then who hears these words of Mine and does them will be like a wise man who built his house on the rock. And the rain fell, and the floods came, and the winds blew and beat on that house, but it did not fall, because it had been founded on the rock. And everyone who hears these words of mine and does not do them will be like a foolish man who built his house on the sand. And the rain fell, and the floods came, and the winds blew and beat against that house, and it fell, and great was the fall of it. (Matthew 7:24–27)

The more I trusted in God, the more secure I felt. The more I learned to care for others, the less I worried about myself. The more I yearned to minister to wolves, the less I feared them. The secret of survival is learning how to die to self. It is making the transformation journey from self to servant by following and imitating Christ. The Bible tells us in Philippians 2:5–8:

Have this mind among yourselves, which is yours in Christ Jesus, who, though He was in the form of God, did not count equality with God a thing to be grasped, but emptied Himself, by taking the form of a servant, being born in the likeness of men. And being found in human form, He humbled Himself by becoming obedient to the point of death, even death on a cross.

X The Truth

All of us have wandered away from the flock occasionally, living selfishly until we found ourselves facing the same type of fork in the road as those inmates staring at the steel bars of their cells. This is where fear exists and causes us to forget the only real way of protection and deliverance. If our minds have been off of God and on ourselves for a long period of time, we can be in the dreadful position of a complete dependence on empty lies. This was most evident to me on the execution night of one condemned inmate who was sadly misdirected. It was a difficult execution for me emotionally and a blunt lesson for me to learn, but it was one I will never forget.

This inmate was sitting in the death house holding cell, acting more nervous than any I had ever seen. He was too nervous to speak or listen to the chaplain. The walk from the death house holding cell to the execution chamber is only about thirty feet. All condemned inmates are heavily escorted for this last, short walk of their lives. The majority of inmates who make that walk seem to have no problem with it and climb up on the death gurney with no assistance. This condemned inmate, however, was a different story. He started the trip by walking very slowly under his own power. He was already jittery, but when he caught sight of the death gurney waiting for him up ahead through the open door at the end of the hallway, he froze in fear. Suddenly the inmate's knees began to wobble, and the poor guy became so scared that he couldn't move except for severe, involuntary trembling. He had to be carried and lifted up onto the death gurney. Even after being entirely strapped down, the inmate was still shaking uncontrollably.

This fellow had spent his entire, lengthy stay on death row believing that this day and moment would never come. He hadn't prepared for it, and he wasn't ready. Many death row inmates have placed so much hope and focus on beating their sentences that they refuse to put their hope in anything else. It is like a cancer patient who has been told he only has a very short time left to live. Instead of spending that time with God in prayer, he sets his mind exclusively on fighting the cancer with medicine, without ever asking the Lord for either physical or eternal healing. Certainly God can and occasionally does miraculously deliver people from a judicial or medical death sentence, but He wants us to know that following the Truth is far more important than a lengthy physical life on earth. Jesus told us in John 18:37: "For this purpose I was born and for this purpose I have come into the world—to bear witness to the truth. Everyone who is of the truth listens to My voice." If we listen to and follow the Truth, we can be ready and prepared for anything, including death.

For the first twenty-five years of my life, I was greatly disturbed by and fearful of death because I did not know the voice of the Shepherd or His Word. Due to my complete ignorance of the Word of God, my concept of the Truth was warped and misdirected. Since hearing the Gospel and believing the Truth in faith, all of the disturbing fears of my life have progressively received comforting direction.

There have been some executions that caused me to become convinced that the person strapped to the death gurney was not at all the one facing the most deadly predicament. It's sobering to watch a convicted criminal dying on the death gurney, knowing that he is immeasurably better off than some of those watching him die. Some nights it is very clear that the condemned inmate has been broken and rebuilt by God and is saved. However, it is sometimes equally clear that some standing there scorning and condemning the inmate are themselves in a far worse state, lost in their godlessness and self-sufficiency. If anyone had a valid reason to be fearful, it would be these people, who put all their trust in this life and in themselves. I was once in a very similar position as some of these witnessing families who professed unbelief. To those who humbly trust Him, God says, "Do not be afraid," yet He reminds the proud and arrogant that they should indeed be afraid (Romans 11:20).

Trusting the Shepherd enough to have no fear was made easier when I understood my position in His sheepfold. It was very comforting when the Shepherd showed me that a God-fearing, repentant murderer is just as much a dearly loved member of His sheepfold as I am. It confirmed my understanding that I am far better off as a weak and dependent sheep whom the Shepherd has to continually rescue from trouble than as the strongest and wisest person outside of the sheepfold.

My position in the sheepfold is to have a heart that is ever dependent on the Shepherd's love and to love the other sheep as He loves me. I know that Jesus came into this world not for the righteous, but for sinners (Matthew 9:12–13). I also know that God is happier about rescuing the one sheep who wandered off than about the ninety-nine who did not (Matthew 18:13). Jesus told the religious people of His day (those that considered themselves better than sinners) that the whores and tax collectors would get into heaven before they would (Matthew 21:31). Ultimately, my sense of security depended on my learning to love both sheep and wolves as Christ does, because perfect love drives out all fear (1 John 4:18).

I viewed my place in prison like I did my place in the sheepfold. This helped me to eventually have an ability to view myself above no one, regardless of what they had done or how they acted. My position in the sheepfold was to fight the good fight with the sword of the Spirit first and foremost. Loving justice and walking humbly before my God (Micah 6:8) gave me greater victories than any physical fights. Successfully wielding the sword of the Spirit while fighting the good fight meant more than just knowing and sharing the Word of God; it meant daily living His Word. Following Jesus meant I had to put off the hypocrisy of focusing on the speck in my brother's eye and be thankful for God's mercy concerning the log in my own eye (Luke 6:41–42).

What mattered more to God than winning any physical fight against assaultive wolves was to love those inmates with a heart of ministry. Being Christlike required that I love my enemies, do good to those who hate me, bless those who curse me, and pray for those who abuse me (Luke 6:27–28). I made steady progress in fighting the good fight by having a heart of ministry toward human wolves. My journey through an atmosphere of constant violence and death became increasingly influenced by lessons of God's grace that I learned while weathering turbulent storms of deep controversial issues.

CHAPTER 10

Shaped by Deterrent Controversies

God transformed my heart, mind, and soul not only through the numerous groups of people with whom I interacted, but also through controversial issues I was forced to deal with, such as whether the death penalty is an effective deterrent to murder. I discovered that when these issues are properly dealt with, they become pivotal in turning all affected lives away from the darkness and toward the light of Christ. Callous disregard of these issues has turned some people toward a life of crime. Yet careful regard has shaped others toward a life of fighting crime. God used my years of being deeply immersed in these issues to spur my heart toward a life of public ministry.

One of the fruits of the Spirit listed in Galatians 5:22–23 is gentleness, a product of not resisting or quenching the Holy Spirit, but following His leading. Whenever the fruit of the Spirit (love, joy, peace, patience, kindness, goodness, faithfulness, gentleness, and self-control) was heavily visible in my life, it became a light of inspiration and influence upon those around me. I prayed constantly for God to enable me to somehow be that light inside the prison. I believe the Lord did enable me to be a light to many, but inside the penitentiary, it certainly was not enough of a deterrent to prevent violent assaults and murders from frequently happening all around me.

As I write this, I am remembering a certain day when I was consciously striving to be the best light possible. It was fifteen years into my career and at a point in my spiritual journey where I had developed many daily habits that helped me be a good witness to those around me. I would wake up early enough to spend time in prayer and read the Word before going to work. The first thing I did after entering my office each day was read the fruits of the spirit in Galatians 5:22–23 to remind myself of what others should see in me. Then I would study the words of Ephesians 6:10 ("Be strong in the Lord and in the strength of His might") inscribed on my coffee mug.

On that particular morning, I was walking across the recreation yard in the middle of the prison, contemplating the counsel of the words on my cup. It was very early in the morning and most of the inmates were still locked up in their cells. The dawning of the day was so peaceful and quiet that I could easily hear the humming of the bumblebees' wings as they moved slowly among the many flower beds at the edge of the yard. The fragrance of all the blooming plants grew stronger as I slowly walked through the middle of these little gardens that were teeming with life. Butterflies of various sizes and colors were gracefully gliding around and appeared to be having a great time.

The birds seemed equally unconcerned that they were in the middle of a dangerous penitentiary. I stopped to watch two mourning doves strolling side by side across the floor of the rose garden. While I was observing them, a bright red cardinal flew past me and perched on a sunflower stem right in front of a brilliant backdrop of white petunias. As the cardinal proceeded to chirp out a soft, cheerful song, I praised God for orchestrating the whole experience. I recalled that when Jesus counseled us to have faith and not worry, He told us to consider the example of the birds and the flowers. I asked God to help me be like them: an inspiring witness that there is a peace in my life more powerful than all of life's challenges. The stillness and tranquility of that moment allowed my heart to drift into an even deeper, intimate prayer of thanks and praise.

Suddenly, the peace and silence was interrupted and shattered by an urgent call being loudly broadcast over our handheld radios. The voice of the control-station officer was hollering for all available officers to report to 5-building immediately. "We've got one down!" she announced. In a split second, dozens of prison guards were scrambling and running across the yard toward 5-building. I heard crash gates slamming shut everywhere to isolate and lock down the rest of the prison. My heart rate was racing in both anticipation and dread of what I would find as I also rushed to the 5-building cellblock. I neared the entrance of the building and was told that an inmate had slit an officer's throat.

As a group of guards rushed past me to confront the assailant, I recognized that their anger was running as hot and fast as their adrenaline. It was understandable. They had just seen their friend rushed away with blood all over his body. I heard that it was a good friend of mine, a highly respected officer. With as much self-control as I could muster while on a full sprint into a lion's den, I counseled them to do whatever they had to do but not to let the inmate take more victims by provoking them into illegal actions that could cost them their jobs. The response team quickly subdued and restrained the assailant without sustaining any injuries themselves or causing any serious damage to the inmate. While everyone was trying to catch their breath and return to a normal heart rate, we learned that the officer was going to be all right. As it turned out, the inmate did some fairly serious damage but slightly missed his target by about an inch—cutting the officer's jaw wide open as he passed by him. The officer was rushed to the hospital to be stitched up, but thanks be to God, he recovered with only a bad scar.

This type of crisis alert happens all too often in the penitentiary and usually comes without warning. But our reaction and response is always predictably the same. When the alarm or cry for help rings out, a distinctively interesting thing happens in the mind and behavior of a prison guard. All personal concerns for safety, self-preservation, or job preservation go out the window. The occurrence of an assault on an officer is always met with swift and extremely serious action to rescue the officer and regain control at all cost.

♀

☒ Death Penalty Debate

Guards are legally authorized to use all force necessary, including deadly force, on inmates who have become an imminent and immediate threat to someone's life. Because of the federally mandated prison reform laws, brutality and injuries inflicted on assaultive inmates beyond what is necessary to rescue and regain control are rare, but many times the necessary force to immobilize a vicious wolf is very serious. In the heat of a life-threatening crisis, the officers' intense focus and priority is on regaining control, not on being sensitive or gentle with the assailant. Therefore, the experience of an assaultive inmate at the moment of confrontation with a rescue squad is seldom without casualties to that inmate's health and sometimes even his life!

All inmates know that the reaction and response of prison guards to a staff assault crisis is always the same. Yet this inmate was completely unconcerned with the possibility of sustaining serious injury or death at the hands of the rescue squad. It was obvious that this inmate was equally indifferent to the possibility of dying by lethal injection for the capital murder he had just attempted. A scenario such as this might appear to be a compelling argument for some anti–death penalty activists that capital punishment is not an effective deterrent.

This experience caused me to study the opposing sides of the huge political controversy over whether the death penalty is a deterrent to capital murder. I wanted to study this topic much further than I had when working on my criminal justice degree. I wanted to go beyond the political academic opinions about the effectiveness of capital punishment as a deterrent. So I studied both social and secular evidence along with the counsel of the Word of God.

I wish that a fear of some form of consequences would have been enough of a deterrent in the mind of this inmate to have saved my friend from the vicious assault, but it was not. I am thankful, however, that a fear of undesirable consequences in the minds of the rescue team kept them from treating the inmate like he treated their fellow officer. I am especially thankful that I had learned to recognize the Shepherd's voice (John 10:4) so I could hear His counsel even in the midst of mayhem as I ran toward 5-building that day. As I was running, other voices were definitely calling out to my old sinful nature, tempting me to react in ungodly ways. I am thankful that my love for the Truth was a definite deterrent to me, preventing me from making inappropriate decisions that would have been unpleasing to my Lord.

My studies quickly convinced me that the argument over the death penalty as an effective deterrent will never end. I also swiftly decided that I would not be seduced into considering one side or the other in this controversy as my enemy. One of the major truths I discovered was that capital punishment may very well be an effective deterrent, but the quest for the best deterrents or the best way to fight the good fight is not answered by wolf control or by wolf extermination—rather, it is by prevention of wolf formation. My heart was moving beyond just crime control toward crime prevention.

How can we prevent our children from growing up to become wolves? And if we succeed, how can we prevent the children down the street from growing up to become the wolves that will victimize our own sons and daughters? Absolute prevention is not possible, because all people make their own decisions and we cannot make those choices for them. There is only one person I can prevent from becoming a wolf, and that is myself. I can't control other people's decisions, but I can influence their decisions by acting as God's representative through my care and love for them.

A common piece of evidence used by some anti–death penalty supporters is statistical data showing lower murder rates in states that do not practice capital punishment. They argue that this proves the death penalty is not a deterrent to committing murder.

As a member of the Texas Death Squad, I found myself constantly blasted by the anti–death penalty activists. They criticized us, claiming that we were not achieving any helpful deterrent, only acting out of motives of vengeance and inappropriate retribution. I gave each of these arguments fair consideration, but continued my studies by considering some evidence from the other side.

Some pro–death penalty people will state that every executed murderer is permanently removed from being a future threat to other potential victims in society. This argument asserts that capital punishment is the ultimate deterrent by protecting society from the convicted murderers who could parole or escape to prey upon society again. Their best example for evidence of this is inmate Kenneth McDuff. McDuff had originally been sentenced to death, but his sentence was commuted to life in prison when the US Supreme Court abolished the death penalty in 1972. McDuff eventually paroled that life sentence and was released back into society where he used his freedom to return to his same murderous habits. Capital punishment was reinstated by the Supreme Court in 1976, so, not long after being released, he worked his way right back to death row again with two more sentences for two separate abductions and murders. It is believed that he also murdered many other young women during this period. Some families of the victims and some pro–death penalty advocates complained that the absence of the death penalty cost these victims their lives.

Please note that I very intentionally state that "some" activists on either side feel or do certain things, because all activists cannot be lumped together as sharing a common mind-set, motive, or worldview. And activists both for and against the death penalty present seemingly valid evidence to support the premise of their perspective about deterrents.

☒ Prevention by Sanctification

I considered all of these differing secular views, but I became increasingly convinced that the most effective deterrent is prevention by sanctification. Knowing, loving, and obeying God's Word is the best deterrent to all violent and destructive behavior. Psalm 119:11

proclaims: "I have stored up Your word in my heart, that I might not sin against You." Although this is great wisdom, the problem is that millions of people have never read or heard one word of Scripture. Even among Christians there is a large percentage of believers that spends little or no time storing God's Word in their hearts. I know this because I was raised Christian but never opened a Bible or read a single sentence of Scripture until I was twenty-five years old. Some of my Christian friends have told me that they were even older before they ever read any Scripture. Those who consistently invest time in God's Word are much less likely to make choices of violence and destruction.

There are over one hundred prison units in the Texas Department of Criminal Justice. Only one of them operates heavily on the model of faith-based ministry and treatment programs. The Carol Vance Unit is set up to offer heavy biblical Christian influence, mainly through Prison Fellowship ministries. The wardens have testified to the impressive facts that the inmates who go through the Prison Fellowship seminars and programs have almost zero disciplinary problems inside the prison and an extremely low relapse rate when they get out of prison. Sadly, this one unit accounts for a very small percentage of the total inmate population in Texas prisons. Even though the light of God's Word is the most effective deterrent, it is the least used.

X Career Criminals

As I considered both secular and biblical views of the deterrent issue, God continued to use my prison experiences to teach me a profound truth about deterrents and the thought process and mind-set of the "career criminal." Approximately 40 percent of the inmates are recidivists (repeat offenders) who have been released from prison before but have returned. Many of these repeat offenders have been in and out of the state penitentiary numerous times, not counting many other stays in the county jails. Whether they are on their second or sixth time in prison, these inmates are mostly career criminals. What I am about to describe is not my opinion, but something I've personally witnessed and learned by listening to offenders' own admissions and by examining their official files, which verify what they explain and describe as their criminal career path.

When a new inmate comes to prison for his first time, he learns a lot through personal experience and by watching and understanding the ways of inmate neighbors all around him:

- *Although there's a lot they don't like about prison, many of them admit that the dry, warm, soft beds they sleep on every night, the three hot nutritionally balanced meals they eat every day, the constant availability of medical and dental care, the daily hot showers, clean clothes, and regular workouts in the gym are luxuries they had little or none of out in the free world.*

- *Many inmates were never legitimately needed or appreciated out in the free world in the way that their prison work supervisors appreciate them in prison. Many work supervisors hate to see valuable, good workers paroled and are actually glad to see them return. Many of these inmates are terrible citizens in the free world but perfect residents in prison.*

- *For many inmates, incarceration is a sure way to escape the mounting stress and pressure of debt, finding and holding a job, and family responsibilities.*

- *There was a lot more money and thrills in selling dope, or pulling off robberies and burglaries, than in the daily grind of a job.*

- *The jails, penitentiaries, and court dockets are so overcrowded that they predictably offer much shorter sentences for a plea bargain of "guilty" to save the state a lot of time and money.*

With all of this in mind, a career criminal not only does not mind getting caught and arrested, but he fully expects to get caught sooner or later. He will fairly accurately imagine his career path of approximately five years in, five years out, five more years back in, then another five out again, with the cycle repeating over and over. The longer an inmate has been out, the more comfortable he is at taking risks, especially if he is feeling increasing pressure from responsibilities or hardships in the free world. The mental image of returning to prison can actually become attractive enough to justify big risks.

Career inmates know the criminal justice system very well and fully understand and calculate the degree of consequences. They know that being arrested for certain crimes committed within a certain degree of parameters will only result in reasonably short sentences. As long as these inmates operate their illegal activities within their self-set boundaries, they really don't mind getting caught eventually, because the trade-off is worth it. They also know they can usually plea-bargain their way out of lengthy sentences even when they qualify for habitual criminal sentencing.

I frequently performed extradition duty for the Texas prison system by flying all over the country to pick up parole violators and take them back to Texas. These offenders had been arrested for some new crime in another state. Those states usually preferred to send the offender back to Texas rather than burdening their own court system with the case. More often than not, while on the trip home sitting next to the inmate on the plane, he would actually express gratitude for being brought back to Texas. The inmate usually explained how he needed to catch up on his medical and dental care, beef up in the gym, and make some fresh new contacts to help him continue his criminal crafts before getting out again.

An example of a boundary across which career criminals will usually not step is the use of a weapon during a burglary, robbery, or other offense. Getting caught with a weapon during such crimes would cause their sentences to be enhanced for a much longer prison term than they want. Career criminals are fully aware that if their robbery victims are killed during their crime, it will not only mess up their career path but also could very easily land them on death row. It is indisputable that thousands of convenience store clerks and other robbery victims are still alive today because the fear of capital punishment is one of the few, but definite, apprehensions or reservations a career criminal carries in his mind as he operates.

Career criminals understand that receiving a life sentence for being a habitual criminal or for murder is always a possibility. Although they do not want such a sentence, they are so institutionalized that spending the rest of their lives in prison does not scare them. They have not only learned how to survive in prison, but they also know how to thrive in the penitentiary world.

The biggest example of a self-set boundary in the minds of career criminals is to never assault or kill an arresting officer. All career criminals know that such an act would end their careers permanently. If the officer dies from the assault, the criminal knows full well that he might face the death penalty. Of the thousands of career criminal offenders who are arrested each year, it is certain that countless law enforcement officers' lives have been saved due to the clear mind-set of the career criminal concerning the death penalty. State and local agencies couldn't pay peace officers enough money to perform their jobs if they weren't protected by effective deterrents against their abusers. Not only do our communities need serious protection from wolves, but crime fighters need more protection than a sidearm. Many would say that if only one police officer's life is saved by the effective deterrent the death penalty carries in the mind of a career criminal, that one life justifies the existence of the death penalty, and that is where the deterrent argument becomes heated.

This leads many to ask the question, whose life needs to be spared? Whose life is more important: the sheep or the wolf? To take a firm stand on one side or the other would be a statement of whose life is more precious. Working so closely with the families of the victims and also with families of the condemned helps me understand how each side of the controversy is offended by the feelings of the other side. It is certain that the death penalty has prevented many a career criminal from committing capital murder, thereby effectively defending and protecting the sanctity of life. But that does not necessarily make anti–death penalty activists opponents of the sanctity of life. Their hearts for mercy and compassion are most honorable, but could this lead to the demise of innocent victims? Does not true love protect the innocent from the evil of an aggressor? Do not the crime fighters who risk their lives to protect us deserve our efforts to protect them? So, what is the appropriate direction for a Christian to follow concerning this issue?

I discovered that this whole deterrent issue is actually very deep, because inmates, like free-world people, are all different. What may be an effective deterrent to one person may be of little or no concern to another. My own two children, when they were growing up, were perfect examples of this. My son, Kent, was deathly afraid of spankings; therefore he rarely ever did anything to deserve one. His little sister, on the other hand, enjoyed testing her parent's patience much more than she feared spankings; therefore she frequently needed them. A deterrent is defined as something that discourages or restrains someone from doing something by instilling fear, anxiety, or doubt. Working with criminals for most of my life has shown me that many inmates not only have zero fear of bodily injury or death, but they actually enjoy defying it. Crime prevention and maintaining control of incarcerated felons can be difficult when you realize that governments have yet to invent a deterrent that strikes fear into the hearts of some hard-core wolves.

Many inmates are reasonably normal people who share the same fears as a free-world person. A great number of these offenders, however, are simply not normal, and they see the world a little (or a lot) differently than most people. I've observed inmates watching television who were not only rooting for the villain but also cheering when an innocent person or a police officer got shot or killed. All of their heroes are wolves, and they are proud of being wolves themselves. I recall an old saying that goes something like this: "The picture that you look at the longest becomes the strongest." Some of these inmates we are trying to deter have been looking at some really weird and different pictures for their entire lives. Understanding criminal minds is challenging, but God led me down the path of dealing with them long enough to help me discover underlying problems that reveal the real deterrent.

☒ Learn Someone's Story

Several years ago, my pastor suggested an idea that became an integral part of my life. He suggested that before we give in to the temptation to judge, condemn, or give up on someone, we should try to learn his or her story. He said that learning someone's story wouldn't justify bad or wrong behavior, and it wouldn't mend the wounds that person may have inflicted on others or on us. It also wouldn't make that person's bad behavior and bad attitude more acceptable, nor would it change his or her heart or make that person more likable. It would, however, give us a fresh dose of patience and compassion. I discovered that as horrible as some inmates' crimes may have been, and as abrasive and hostile as their attitudes still were, God loved them. Learning their stories gave me a glimpse into how God sees them in His grace and mercy. This became another powerful application of Jesus' counsel to be wise as serpents but gentle as doves when dealing with human wolves. It helped me understand the absolute necessity of both godly wisdom and Christlike gentleness in accurately considering the appropriateness of any crime-deterrent efforts.

As I started to do some digging to learn the stories of inmates, I discovered many common factors and conditions. A great number of these inmates had been trying to cope with a physically and emotionally abusive childhood by turning to rebellion. Thousands of inmates struggled to deal with a lack of identity and purpose all their lives because they were raised without a father at home to guide them, so they turned to dope dealers or gang leaders for their father figures. For many, the only role models they had to follow and emulate were ex-convicts and criminals in their neighborhoods. Along their life journeys, most of them had been taught ways to ingrain in their minds some very good-sounding or convincing justifications for their inappropriate actions. They were trained to blame society or others for what and whom they had become. They were therefore trapped in a downward tailspin, because they had never been taught any principles of personal accountability and responsibility.

I understand that we are all responsible for our own life choices, and I know that many children have survived and overcome bad influences. I have seen the children of criminals grow up to become preachers, and I have also seen the children of preachers grow up to become criminals. Society is not totally responsible for the influences that cause children to become wolves, but we can certainly make a lot of bad contributions. Beyond the obvious bad influences of the glorification of alcohol and drug abuse and violence on television and movies, even the typical, average community can make many detrimental contributions to the minds of impressionable young people.

The average high school or junior high closely resembles a prison in many ways. Aside from the physical resemblance of the buildings and the constant need for roaming security guards, students and inmates alike must survive the daily threats and bad influences from mental, physical, sexual, and verbal abuse, along with drug dealers and gangs. Just like with prisons, the larger the school, the more dangerous and intimidating it is. If the crime deterrent of a solid Christian influence is completely absent from a young person's life, he or she is extremely vulnerable to dangerous influences that can harden his or her heart.

The hard, mean character I saw in many inmates was a face they built as firmly as they could. It usually hid the fear and pain they were ashamed to let show. The abrasive, defiant personality common in so many of them was often an attitude of self-reliance they developed because of neglect and abandonment in their younger years. But while it may have helped them get tougher, it also built a hard shell around their hearts, which prevented any potential for growth opportunities leading to intellectual or spiritual maturity.

By learning and understanding this, God helped me to be more effective in dealing with inmates in ways that contributed to their only chance for deterring their criminal behavior. I never had to dwell on the inmates' stories very long to understand that some of them were bound by serious strongholds and had no hope for a breakthrough outside of Jesus Christ. Many inmates were suppressed by the mentality and understanding that they had made a mess of their lives, and they were convinced in their hearts that they were losers and worthless. Several inmates felt that the whole world had counted them out and given up on them. Many of them couldn't see past their personal estimation of how much they had let their mother down, let their spouse and kids down, and let themselves down.

As I said earlier, sometimes broken is good. So often these broken lives were extremely fertile ground for the life-giving touch of God through a prison ministry worker who, by God's timing, did indeed break through and share the good news that they could start over brand new in Jesus Christ! So often all they needed was for just one of these ministers to explain that Jesus Christ could and would take their broken and wasted life and completely rebuild and restore it. The one and only way they ever would have broken their career cycle and their bondage to a damaged self-image was to be led to understand that through complete surrender to Jesus, they did not have to walk out of prison in the same condition in which they walked in. Just when an inmate is certain that nothing good could possibly come out of his life, Jesus knocks on the bars of his cell door through the instrument of a prison ministry worker who explains that Christ came not for the righteous but for sinners. Deciding whether the death penalty is a deterrent is not nearly as important as deciding that Jesus is the only real solution to criminal behavior! Whether the Word is shared with a young person before he or she falls into criminal behavior or with an inmate who already has, Christ is the solution.

☒ Is Hell a Deterrent to Sin?

Earlier in this chapter, I offered some insight to understanding the career criminal's mind-set. Those thought processes may be new and even shocking to some, but I have found that there are actually interesting similarities between the mind-set of a career criminal and the typical thinking of the average American citizen and the average Christian in this country.

My quest for the answer to the question about the death penalty being a deterrent to murder might best be answered with this question: is hell a deterrent to sin? The answer is the same for both questions. Sometimes it is, sometimes it isn't. I know some people who have openly admitted that they believe in God, yet they also admit that they completely reject Him and hate Him. I know that there are thousands of others who feel that same way and consciously choose to spend eternity separated from God. Even us sheep, whom the Shepherd has saved from the jaws of the devil, should appreciate our deliverance by Jesus on the cross enough to never sin again, but we sin anyway. The amazing power of God's grace is recognized when we realize we can never attain sinless perfection. The Law of God acts as a deterrent by informing us of the wages of sin as a curb, a mirror, and a guide toward justification and sanctification.

A criminal who rationalizes that some rewards are worth taking a certain degree of risk for while others are not can be compared to any of us in some ways. Unfortunately, I have to admit that I am occasionally guilty of "allowing" myself to slip into some sinful behavior while I set definite limits on myself regarding other acts. In the same way that career criminals operate within their self-set limitations, Romans 3:23 reveals that all people apparently feel there are wages of certain sins that are worth paying the consequence for. All believers risk the death of a relationship or the death of some blessings from God by occasionally wandering away from the flock into wolf country. In much the same way that some inmates become experts at coming up with justifications for their behavior, I am guilty of that same mind-set when I am not immediately convicted of and repentant for my decisions to sin. Despite my understanding of the wages of sin, I have an embarrassing problem. When I desire to sin strongly enough, I can manipulate my conscience until it no longer protects me. This is often referred to as quenching the Spirit.

One of my friends was a longtime Texas state representative. I was in his office one day, asking him some questions about ethics, when he told me a story that I will never forget. He explained that he once wanted to enter into a business venture that he felt might damage his political credibility. He approached Congresswoman Barbara Jordan for her opinion about his dilemma. He carefully worded his question to Ms. Jordan in a manner that would hopefully show integrity. She answered, "You know, Congressman, it completely amazes me how often people will ask questions . . . the answer to which, they already know."

Her brief answer brought him to his knees in conviction of his attempt at self-manipulation. Praise God for friends with the courage and character to hold us accountable to the truth! There aren't very many friends like that out there. Sometimes, that is by our deliberate choice. Once we have become good at lying to ourselves, we will almost always try to complete the paving of our comfortable path into sin by seeking the support of someone who isn't really a friend at all.

My sinful nature is stronger than my ability to resist it by myself. The hand of God in answered prayer is the only true friend I can always count on for this help. The problem is that if I don't face my weaknesses, I won't ask for His help. If there is no prayer, there will be no answered prayer. God's helping hand will occasionally come in the form of a faithful servant whom He gives me as one of my friends. When my mind is set on sin, however, it wants a different kind of support. Knowing my own struggle with manipulating my conscience to allow myself to sin helped me understand the serious obstacles our society faces in pursuit of judicial deterrents.

The justice system is laden with the burden of attempting to reveal the truth among the craftiest of manipulators. I have known inmates who were highly skilled at beating a polygraph test. They taught me that it is simply the "art" of firmly believing your own lie. Getting others to believe it as well is another art. Judges have their work cut out for them! When wolves finally get caught and find themselves facing a jury, what happens? An attorney dresses them up in a business suit and grooms them to the point that their own friends would not even recognize them. They then conduct themselves in a manner that pulls on the heartstrings of the jury until the jury sympathizes with their plight and hopefully believe their defense or justifications.

Each of us does the same thing whenever we consciously recruit the support of our friends in justification of our inclinations to sin. This justification at its full-blown worst extreme is when people eventually manage to convince themselves that God does not even exist. Once people have enabled themselves to believe this, they can completely discount their sinful actions. Now they can feel that they are merely ruffling the feathers of a conservative special interest group known as Christians.

There is a segment of society that is terribly frightened, but not frightened of human wolves. What these people are afraid of is the Truth. Unfortunately it is not a healthy, reverent fear of God; rather it is a fear of influence from the Spirit they have worked so hard to quench and cover up. I found that there can be no deterrent to any crime or any sin whenever the perpetrator is able to remove all guilt and responsibility from his or her mind. A wolf comfortable with and committed to self-destructive behavior can only be deterred by obtaining a healthy fear of God. Even when a wolf is enabled by the Holy Spirit to believe the truth of the Gospel, the Means of Grace God uses to offer His truth are still resistible. God never forces wolves to fear Him, but pursues them through Spirit-led hearts that share and "live" His Gospel. God's persistent love often breaks through the darkness that had prohibited stubborn wolves from recognizing the lies that caused them to resist and reject His grace. But even the brightest light of the most convincing truth will not make sense to those who are spiritually dead. Those who have rejected the Light and eclipsed it with their love of sin are on the wide and easy path of no deterrence. Anyone who is still bothered by conscience when the Holy Spirit convicts him or her of sin, however, can certainly be blessed by God's instruments of deterrence.

X̄   The Grace of God

I have been blessed with a son who likes to spend time with me. He wants and seriously appreciates my input on the concerns that arise in his life. Once, back when he was still a teenager, he wanted to ask me some questions about eternal rewards and consequences. I told him that he was a much better person than I was, so if good behavior helped someone get to heaven, he would get there before I would. Then, before I could continue, he hit me with a really powerful question. He asked me, "Dad, do you think a guy like me deserves to go to hell?" After a brief pause and a deep sigh, I answered, "Son, we all do." I explained that all of us have occasionally chosen to commit acts of sin that deserve the sentence of hell. If it weren't for Jesus' atoning sacrifice to save us and give us the ability to repent and receive His mercy and grace, we would all get what we truly deserve. If all of us sheep would ask the same question and dwell on the answer, we would enjoy the greatest deterrent to going astray.

I often dwelt on the words of Job 5:17: "Blessed is the one whom God reproves." In this contrast to typical thinking I found great wisdom that helped deter me from straying. Any interruption to our plans or activities that helps to wean us from our fleshly corruption and deter us from self-destruction is a huge blessing. Even the most painful and uncomfortable experience has priceless value if it brings us to our knees, draws us closer to God, and ultimately improves our condition.

Those who have never had the blessing of being raised by loving earthly parents yearn for a father to correct and discipline them. It is a magnificent blessing indeed that our father God loves us enough to correct us (Hebrews 12:5–11). No deterrent is too severe once we learn that God's grace is in greater abundance than the consequences of our sinful disobedience. Deterrent experiences are blessings that we cannot afford to waste. God wants to use them for good in shaping the convictions of our hearts.

I struggled for years weighing the influences that tugged my heart back and forth. It took me an embarrassingly long time to finally trust God enough to realize that the answer to finding the best deterrent options will always be biblical at the core (Deuteronomy 28). I am thankful that many criminals fear capital punishment. I am even more thankful that millions of us Christians reverently fear God enough to choose obedience over sin most of the time. Consequences for criminal behavior are necessary, but the most effective deterrent is not any certain type of penalty; it is prevention, through sharing the love of the Shepherd. When we are a reflection of Jesus to a wayward wolf, the influence of our living testimony is the best deterrent against that person's notion to stray into destructive behavior. When we understand that the only real deterrent from any sinful behavior is to love God more than we love ourselves and to consciously choose to honor the limits and direction He gives, we will be wise as serpents. When we trust the Lord so much that we recognize His voice and praise Him even in the midst of mayhem or uncomfortable discipline, we will be as innocent and gentle as doves.

Being mindful of the serpent/dove principle guided me when political controversies tugged my heart in different directions, trying to respectfully consider the passionately felt ideas of both sides. Proper application of the serpent/dove principle required interpreting in light of the whole of God's Word. Whether it was read or preached, I understood that I needed to absorb God's Word and follow it. Rather than being torn by mixed emotions from all of the political activists

I encountered, I would read, pray, and let Scripture interpret Scripture. Ultimately, I was always blessed for doing so. I often prayed the prayer of David from Psalm 143: "Make me know the way I should go . . . teach me to do Your will, for You are my God!" (vv. 8 and 10). He often taught me His will and showed me His way by humbling me and revealing more of my own personal weaknesses.

The political controversy lessons taught me to humbly accept the fact that God allows our lives to be filled with a mixture of pain and pleasure, of defeat and victory, of dark valleys and bright mountaintops. It takes both good times and bad times to attain maturity. The closer I walked with Christ, the more I became tempted to trade my prison career for enrollment in a theological seminary. All of the Bible scholars in the world, however, could never have taught me the powerful life lessons God showed me through the countless dark valleys in the belly of the beast of the penitentiary. In one of the most antagonistic and brutal classrooms imaginable, I kept learning to look beyond the constant distractions and focus intently on the lessons the Shepherd was teaching.

At the beginning of my prison employment, I chose all the wrong teachers and quickly learned to deal with dangerous wolves by being meaner and more vicious than they were. By the grace of God, through brokenness and His discipline, I was enabled to recognize the voice of the Good Shepherd and follow Him as my instructor from that point forward. Despite that change, most experiences I continued to encounter were still life threatening, and all of them were life altering. Throughout this book I have been sharing many of those experiences. Reading through them may feel like an emotionally traumatic journey because that is exactly what it was for me. Each step of the journey challenged my understanding of God's will and my perception of the truth. Each chapter has explored a different aspect of suffering for those affected by capital murder or capital punishment, and I struggled through every dramatic episode to determine right from wrong and the truth from a lie.

My quest to know the truth about deterrents caused my heart to be tugged in different directions at every controversial fork in the road by influences that were utterly compelling but diametrically opposed to each other. I never knew what arguments would win each tug-of-war for the convictions of my heart, but my resolute conviction that God's Word would ultimately reveal the answer proved true. One of the greatest blessings we humans have is that God's grace is freely given and offered, yet it is also resistible. Because human beings have the freedom to reject God's grace, no deterrent is completely effective. This truth would be driven deeper into my soul in the experiences that I was yet to encounter.

CHAPTER 11

Shaped by Justice/Injustice Controversies

As I neared the twenty-year mark in my prison career and was well into my forties, I suddenly needed glasses for the first time in my life. While trying to renew my driver's license at the Texas Department of Transportation office, I failed my eye test and was not permitted to drive until I fixed the problem. I had to face the cold, hard reality that I was getting old and my body wasn't exactly what it used to be. At forty-five years of age, my eyes needed corrective lenses, but my heart had attained clarity of vision that was far greater than ever before.

By that time, I was able to look back and see that the daily demands of prison administration had grown much more intense yet somehow more manageable. I perceived that as I grew closer to the Lord, my battles against evil had grown more volatile, but the different kinds of wolves I faced were more easily overcome. I realized that as my ability to know and wield the sword of the Spirit increased, the demand to use it had grown proportionately. I was aware that in the final trimester of my career, I had a lot less physical fights with inmates but considerably more spiritual assaults. Many of those assaults came from that certain segment of society that had varying motives and agendas. The capital punishment arena was a hotbed of numerous controversies and a highly visible platform from which people could effectively draw attention to themselves, broadcast their opinions, and recruit support for their cause. I was one of their targets. My eyes didn't work as well as they used to, but I could easily see that I needed to cling closer to the Shepherd than ever before to retain the truth amidst a barrage of differing opinions about what was right and wrong.

After my physical life on this earth is over, I would like to be remembered as a sheep who was a reflection of the Good Shepherd in the way I responded to constant spiritual assaults. I would also like to leave a legacy of being a diligent Bible teacher whose students are still bearing fruit from the truth they learned in God's Word. I might, however, be remembered by some for giving an entirely different type of teaching and training.

Over the years, as different states chose to begin the practice of capital punishment or changed their method of execution to lethal injection, they came to Texas to be trained in this procedure. I helped train numerous agencies from other states, as well as the federal correctional agents who executed the Oklahoma City bomber, Timothy McVeigh. Normally, it would be an honor to be considered the experts in the country and an even greater honor to be sought as consultants, teachers, and trainers, but in this profession, it was a pretty dubious distinction.

Some agencies timed their trip to Texas so that they could be present when we had multiple executions in one week in order to get the most training from their visit. I spent a lot of time with some of those agents and would often discuss the similarities and differences of the political climates of our states. I learned that citizens from virtually every state in the union fight over the exact same issues. Currently, thirty-one of the fifty states in the US use capital punishment, but the battle over this controversial practice is continuously disputed in every state.

Most states have classified the act of taking the life of another person into various categories, definitions, and degrees of murder or homicide, according to the severity of intent or culpability. Varying lengths of prison terms are usually established and implemented according to the circumstances involved or surrounding the specific combination of acts committed during the crime. But what about the murderers whom society classifies as the most dangerous wolves of all? How should society deal with someone found guilty of capital murder? There are many different areas of concern and responsibility to be considered with this question, and each one has caused controversy throughout society and within my heart.

☒ Judicial Inequality

One accusation that was constantly being thrown in my face was that I might possibly be participating in the execution of innocent men. As many as one out of three executed inmates here in Texas die insisting that they are innocent. Unfortunately, it has been proven that some people have indeed been wrongly convicted of capital murder in this country. The public must understand, however, that there is a big difference in being wrongly convicted and being innocent. Many capital murder convictions have been overturned due to later findings of inappropriate proceedings in the trial or the gathering of evidence, but I believe that completely innocent people actually being convicted and executed in this country in recent times would be extraordinarily rare and infrequent.

I knew the possibility existed, but I would not allow myself to dwell on it because it was not my business to determine guilt in those cases. I knew I was not on the jury that heard the evidence leading to the conviction and sentencing. Therefore, any opinions from anyone who was not on that jury, including myself, would be completely speculative and based on considerably less evidence than the jury had to make their decision. Most condemned inmates eventually admitted their guilt. But of those who held fast to their claims of innocence, I read the hearing records, spoke to witnesses, and listened to both the prosecuting and defense attorneys. It was almost always unanimously agreed that the evidence of guilt was overwhelming. I therefore had no choice but to trust the decision handed down by the jurors as I carried out the duty of execution for the state.

When I was studying criminal justice in college, some professors taught that we would be better off letting ninety-nine guilty people go before we found one innocent person erroneously guilty. Other professors taught the exact opposite, so I learned early on that this issue would not be an easy one. No one can deny that it would be a horrible tragedy to execute an innocent man. Whether such a consideration carries enough weight to abolish the death penalty is for the lawmakers to decide. I've never sat on a jury for a capital murder trial, but I would imagine it would be a tremendous emotional burden of responsibility to be absolutely convinced and certain of guilt as jurors cast their votes, so I have to believe those people take their decision very seriously. Our country has to have a method of enforcing the law, and our current judicial system seems as good or better than any other nation's in guaranteeing an accused person a full extent of procedural due process rights for a fair trial. I am sure that jurors and public servants in the judicial process do not like the frequency of executions any more than the anti–death penalty crowd.

Another issue that was often shouted in my face was judicial inequality. Some voiced strong concerns because there were disproportionate numbers of death sentences given to minorities and lower-income people. Is this a problem of unequal enforcement? Is this a problem of biased or prejudiced jurors? Whenever the answer to either of these questions is yes, we are faced with a horrible injustice. Our country has made tremendous progress but is still working hard to emerge from an ugly history of severe racial and ethnic differentiation. A society that has been plagued by any degree of social or institutional discrimination will suffer in every aspect of that society, including judicial injustices. Each individual perpetrator of a capital murder must be indiscriminately tried on the basis of that person's criminal behavior without regard to race or social class. If members of a jury cannot separate the perpetrator from his or her race or social class, then they are in need of a change of attitude. Such a change of attitude is only possible with a complete transformation of the hearts of men. This is not achievable by legislation. Only God can change a heart through the work of His Holy Spirit. The only hope for social reform is for humans to love God enough to want to know His will and please Him. Some of the most dangerous wolves are not those who physically commit murder, but rather those who hate their fellow man (1 John 3:15).

On many execution nights, the anti–death penalty activists were very vocal and demonstrative in their condemnation of capital punishment procedures. Bullhorns were used to angrily shout and broadcast their accusations that the members of the death squad were murderers. A common chant compared death row to Auschwitz and Buchenwald. If someone actually believes that the actions of our government are comparable to the atrocities of the Holocaust, I do not blame them for being so angry and vocal, but I thank God that these loud accusations are only gross exaggerations. I will certainly be the first to admit that governments can abuse their authority and become a monstrous beast. History reveals tragic examples of many governments that became the most vicious and merciless wolves. I am thankful that if executions have to be carried out, our country allows them only after long and complete exhaustion of all legal procedures and appeals.

For whatever the reason, the pro–death penalty folks rarely made an appearance in Huntsville, but when they showed up, their feelings were just as emotional and strong as their opposition. There were times when it would have been easy for me to take sides with the pro–death penalty crowd, because I knew most of the details and gruesome facts describing and surrounding each crime. I have watched condemned inmates not only admit to being guilty, but brag about, laugh about, and take great pride in their crimes. It would have been very easy for me to allow myself to become outraged and hateful toward some condemned inmates because their crime descriptions were often so horrible, grotesque, and brutally savage that it turned my stomach. On some execution nights I had to pray extra hard to not get caught up in that trap. To do so would have caused me to enter an execution duty with a condemning spirit and a smug, self-righteous attitude by comparing myself to the inmate. For this reason I never even studied an inmate's rap sheet until the last possible moment. I definitely did not like some of them, but I loved all of them. With God's help, I avoided elevating myself above any of them. I couldn't afford to; my sins needed to be covered by Jesus' atoning blood just as much as the condemned inmate's.

I did not have to study some rap sheets. Some death row inmates were notorious criminals because their crimes and trials were highly publicized. When all of the gruesome details of a crime were widely known by everyone, there was even greater temptation to lean toward hate. In the last couple years of my career, we received two new inmates on death row who were admittedly guilty of an unbelievably horrible and merciless murder near Jasper, Texas. They had chained a man to the back of their truck and dragged him to death. When his body was discovered, it was in several pieces. It was admittedly a racially motivated hate crime. Some people told me: "I'll bet you can't wait to kill those guys." I was indeed outraged by the crime and angry at the offenders when I thought about the crime, but I never looked forward to any execution. We all sin against others, and we deserve the anger of those we offend. Murderers deserve our anger. But our anger towards them is righteous and just only when it doesn't linger or carry us into self-righteousness and hate (Matthew 5:21–22). Instead, our anger towards them should be redirected to the devil, who is controlling them. Our emotions should motivate us to responsibly confront evil and cling to the Shepherd for help to forgive, but not lure us into hate and a heart of vengeance.

X Having a Godly Attitude

There was one death row inmate whose crime and remorseless attitude were so despicable that the arrival of his execution date severely tested my heart. A father and his young son were enjoying a peaceful camping and fishing trip in the woods of East Texas when this human wolf walked into their campsite. I will not describe the atrocious and detestable things he did to them before and while he killed them. My heart is shaken and grieved as I write this and recall all of the details. I knew that I was teetering dangerously on the edge between righteous and unrighteous anger that day. I recall praying fervently for a heart that was as gentle as a dove.

God often rescued me from self-destructive emotions and taught me profound lessons through radio preachers, and He did so that day with perfect timing. I recognized the voice of the Shepherd speaking to me through a preacher who was teaching a lesson from Mark 7:24–30, where Jesus was confronted by a Gentile woman. The Word tells us that she was a Greek from Syrophoenicia, which was not only a pagan region but also the home of a notorious wolf pack of godless oppressors of Israel. Jesus did not call her a wolf, but He did refer to her and her people as dogs. The Syrophoenician woman deserved Jesus' anger. However, she humbly accepted her position of truly being an unacceptable dog. The reason Jesus confronted the woman this way was to teach people like me that until and unless I learn to approach Jesus as she did—in humility as a poor, needy sinner—I am no less of a dog than she. Jesus had mercy on her despite her unworthiness, and I must do the same.

This lesson not only humbled me but also caused me to feel a tremendous responsibility. As a believer in Christ, my attitude is supposed to be contagious. If I displayed an attitude of love and humility, it would be an influence to all of the people around me on tense execution nights. When I faced that angry segment of society that attacked me with their nonbiblical worldviews about law and justice, I had an opportunity to be a loving, godly influence to them. My influence was critical because the people around me were not only sensitive, but they were also media targets who would influence their community, their state, and ultimately the direction of the nation.

⊠ Freedom

In our country, the authorities who make the decisions to allow or to abolish capital punishment are appointed or elected by the people. Therefore, the decision to grant our government the power to take the lives of its own citizens by execution is ultimately decided by "the people." In a civilized, democratic society, how much power should a government have over its people? This question, with all of its many possible answers, comprises the basis for all divisions and disagreements between political parties, special interest groups, and cultural or social classes in America. The challenge lies in that "the people" are all separate individuals, each with the freedom to think and express their personal opinions independently.

The term *freedom* is a refreshing word and a welcome sound in anyone's ear, but its meanings and interpretations are as numerous as the individuals themselves. Different individual interpretations of what freedom should mean are the cause of the most bitter and heated controversial disputes on the subject of capital punishment.

Simply the ability to participate in a controversial dispute concerning the government is a precious freedom. We all witnessed the exact opposite in Afghanistan and Iraq before their liberation. We saw citizens in those countries being executed for the slightest hint of disagreement with their government. At that same time here in the US, however, we saw many Americans not only being allowed to protest against our government, but even being given police protection while they did so.

I grew to greatly appreciate and constantly give thanks for the gift of freedom when I worked in the penitentiary. Prison inmates not only do not have the freedom to leave the prison, but they also have virtually no freedom of choice on the inside. The state decides when they wake up, when they go to bed, where they work, when they eat, what they eat, when they recreate, what they wear, when they shower, when and if they get visits, and virtually every other aspect of their lives.

For the rest of us, any type of freedom is always a double-edged sword. The side that liberates pleases people. The side that protects scares people. Let's examine the realities of this truth. No group of citizens will ever be able to collectively agree on any justice system to which they have to submit. We are all innately aware of right and wrong and are prone to hide our wrongdoings, because God made us to know that our own wrongs are without excuse (Romans 1:18–22). As a consequence, there will always be at least some fear of justice. The very thought of "getting what we deserve" frightens everyone.

I found that some of my opponents cling to a nonbiblical view of justice to help them pretend that they are free from one more source of accountability. I have also found that they really know in their heart that they have only increased their bondage, because opposing the truth does not make it any less true. That's why the only true and complete freedom is in Christ.

Acceptance of Jesus as Lord over every area of my life was my only hope of not getting what I truly deserved. If I had received punishment in proportion to the sins I've committed, I would have been destroyed a long time ago. I found that when I stopped resisting Christ and surrendered to Him as my Shepherd, I instantly felt the freedom of His mercy. That is why Jesus told us: "If the Son sets you free, you will be free indeed" (John 8:36).

Freedom in Christ is the ultimate freedom. It is just the opposite of worldly freedom. In Christ, the more we give of ourselves to Him, the more freedom we experience, feel, and enjoy. In this world, however, the more power we give to our government, the less power and freedom we have as citizens. The more we empower the government to protect us and take care of us, the less power we personally have to protect and take care of ourselves. When does the government have too much power? To fully examine this we must consider several other questions:

- *Does freedom mean that we live comfortably because we empower our government to protect its citizens from criminals by extensive law enforcement and stern deterrent consequences for crimes?*

- *Does freedom mean that we can comfortably enjoy our citizenship knowing we won't be oppressed and improperly treated by our government because we have limited and restricted its power to enforce laws and impose penalties?*

- *At what point have the people sacrificed too much of their personal freedom by giving the government too much power?*

- *At what point have the people given themselves so much freedom that the lack of accountability breeds dangerous, self-destructive social chaos?*

Some people, I have learned, are anti–death penalty activists because they feel most threatened by the government and want to limit its power; some people are pro–death penalty activists because they feel most threatened by individuals and want to empower the government to control them. There is obviously no universal agreement among "the people" regarding the answers to these and countless other freedom-related issues. As long as the citizens of this country have the freedom and the right to voice their opinions and vote for changes, the degree of power the government has will be forever transforming back and forth. I fully expect that capital punishment could be abolished and reinstated several times in this century.

⊠ The Light of Christ

During the presidential elections of 2000 and 2004, I saw our entire nation caught up in frustrating, confusing, and controversial fights that divided our nation quite seriously for long periods of time. Not only was the nation sharply divided on issues they were voting on, but the divisions were amazingly even. As each issue dragged on, there seemed to be only lose-lose situations as half of the country was deadlocked in a type of tug-of-war against the other half. In each election, I saw many people grow weary of the lengthy confrontations, yet thousands of Americans became increasingly devoted to their causes and fought even harder for their sides. Each side was obviously convinced that their beliefs were correct; therefore, they were immovable and uncompromising in defense of their feelings.

As I observed both of these ordeals going on, they reminded me a lot of the constant environment of the capital punishment world. We see the same type of division between the activists for and against the death penalty. Both appear to be quite equal in numbers, in support, and in the depth of their convictions. Each side appears equally committed to the tenacious pursuit of its goal and equally passionate about its beliefs. Both are totally convinced with every fiber of their being that they are correct. How does a Christian know which side of a controversy is right? I learned to take the tough questions to the Shepherd by comparing differing opinions to His Word.

An example of this *pro* versus *anti* controversy at its worst came on the execution date of inmate Gary Graham. Inmate Graham was sentenced to death for a May 1981 robbery and murder in Houston. While inmate Graham sat on death row for over eighteen years, his case became a highly publicized center of heated debate between those for and against the death penalty. Several Hollywood stars and political personalities became highly vocal on behalf of inmate Graham. As the execution date grew closer, extremists vowed to show up at the prison armed and prepared for violence. Texas state law enforcement agencies literally prepared for war on that day.

On June 22, 2000, Graham's scheduled execution day, activists from both sides gathered around the Walls Unit in massive numbers. I would imagine that many of you reading this might have seen portions of this event on the news, because the media coverage was expansive. Never had this controversy become so explosive and hostile as it did on that day.

Thousands of demonstrators assembled in front of the penitentiary. True to their vow, many protestors brought rifles and shotguns and waived them in the air as they marched around the prison for hours. The confrontation between the two crowds was so hostile it appeared that a bloody war was about to take place.

The street and lawn in front of the Walls Unit are frequently crowded with protestors for and against capital punishment on execution days.

Photo courtesy of Texas Department of Criminal Justice.

My wife, Jill, always prayed for me during every execution, and on this night she was praying for me with an intensity and passion like never before. As she looked out the windows of our home, she saw the huge, angry crowds armed with guns. She was behind closed doors, but the roaring noise of the crowd was so loud she felt swallowed up in their midst. Jill prayed without ceasing for hours on end, crying out to God for my protection and for a peaceful resolution to the raging conflict.

The pressing crowd was kept at a reasonably safe distance from the front door of the prison by a show of force from a tremendous number of Texas State Troopers poised in full riot gear. They were seriously outnumbered by the protestors but were effectively ominous to the angry crowd. I am convinced that their presence and tactical deployment was the supremely answered prayer that prevented many protestors from giving their lives for the cause during that event. Tensions and emotions flared and erupted violently all evening from both sides of the controversy, and it was obvious that numerous activists were prepared to pay a very high price in support of their beliefs. As I escorted the witnesses through the ocean of news media and across the street, I was thanking God for the thick barrier of police riot squads, swat teams, and low-flying police helicopters between the angry crowd and us.

We watched numerous outbreaks of violent confrontations that were quickly swarmed by police and contained in time to prevent tragedy. Although the eruption of a major bloody war seemed imminent all evening, Jill's prayers were answered and nothing more than small skirmishes actually occurred. As I observed all of this happening, and later watched it on our crowd-scanning video recordings, I looked closely at all of those who were creating disturbances. I was thankful that the worst possible catastrophes were avoided. I was glad to find that none of those acting in an unruly or disruptive way were doing so in the name of Christianity. It is honorable and necessary to stand up for what we believe in. But even so, this should be done peacefully and in order (1 Corinthians 14:40).

We Christians have a responsibility and right to work for justice in society and should indeed show our concerns, but only as long as we are more effective as prayer warriors for the cause than as political warriors. Overzealous dragon slayers could become dragons themselves if they are not careful and prayerful!

A Christian leader God used as a profound influence on me by demonstrating a perfect example of responsibly working for justice is Dr. James Dobson. In defense of biblical standards of morality, he has squared off in serious debate against numerous "dragons" over the years. One of the most valuable lessons I learned from Dr. Dobson was how to have and display the mind of Christ while battling dragons. I am convinced that more people have been blessed by watching Dr. Dobson's amazing display of peaceful self-control and his love for his enemies than by listening to his persuasive arguments. Dr. Dobson has faced violent and abusive verbal assaults from his opponents, yet he always responds to them with gentle, sincere loving concern for their souls. I needed his Matthew 10:16 example of how to properly represent Christ while defending the truth.

As a Christian called to serve both God and country in the controversial role of inmate executions, my primary responsibility was the same responsibility held by every Christian. Jesus said that we must let our light shine before men so they may see what we do and give glory to God (Matthew 5:16). Could people see what I did in the execution chamber and give glory to God?

If I truly know God, love Him with all of my heart, soul, mind, and strength, and serve both Him and my neighbor above myself, I will reflect the light of Christ. But could I reflect the light of Christ in the death house? In that dark, dreadful place I knew it would be an extraordinary challenge, but I serve an extraordinary God and I saw many people glorify Him there.

Even in the most unlikely times and places, if the light of Christ is shining through His people, the hopeless find hope, the brokenhearted are restored, and hard, hateful hearts are softened. I have seen the hardest hearts melt like wax in the death house and give glory to God. I have seen the smallest sheep in the darkest corners of the prison reflect the light of Christ brighter than you could imagine.

I loved attending inmate chapel services, because I could always tell that it was one of the most precious hours of their week. For this one hour they could focus intently on Christ and love their brother uninhibitedly. In that chapel they were temporarily liberated from the con games and pressures that constantly threatened them. I could easily see a glow in their faces because they were feeling and sharing the power of God's presence.

I noticed that their light was far brighter, however, when they were the lone beacon of God's grace on their cellblock or at their work assignment. All the other inmates recognize that because of one Christian in their midst, not only do they have one less wolf to beware of, but that Christian also represents a bright ray of hope that they, too, can possibly have that peace and joy. I can assure you that God is glorified by all who see what this one sheep does.

☒ The Lord Weighs the Heart

While writing this chapter, my wife, Jill, and I traveled to Dallas to visit a church that my senior pastor recommended. It was a cold, rainy day, which slowed our travel speed, and when we finally arrived at the church, it was almost time for the service to begin. It was a huge church, and the only parking spaces available were at the far end of a parking lot that seemed to be the same size as Dallas/Fort Worth International Airport. The thought of how cold and wet we would be by the time we walked all the way to the church entrance dampened our spirits, but we didn't want to be late, so we started the long trek.

Before we got too far, two men with large umbrellas came running up to meet us. With huge smiles and warm, friendly greetings, they thanked us for coming and held the umbrellas over us as we walked. I felt kind of bad because since they were holding the umbrellas over us, it meant they got wet. Yet despite the fact that their hair, suits, and shoes were soaked and rain was dripping off their faces, the men were smiling, laughing, and talking about how excited they were that we had come to share in worshiping the Lord with them that morning. When we reached the entrance of the sanctuary, the men thanked us once more, shook our hands, then turned and dashed back out into the rain. I remember thinking that not only were those poor guys totally cold and wet, but they would also miss the service. Then it hit me—they are the service!

As I pondered that thought, I stood and watched the men running through the rain. I realized that those men were living out their faith so effectively that the light of Christ in them had ignited and fanned into flame the spirit in me that I had allowed to be dampened by the rain. I was tremendously blessed, but I was also convicted because I knew that their level of selfless, loving service to God and their neighbor far exceeded my own. I was thankful that the Lord had allowed me to experience His love through those men so that I could humbly ask the Holy Spirit to help me love the sheep and wolves in my life that powerfully.

Jesus said in the Gospel of Matthew, "Love your enemies" (5:44). In the Gospel of John, we are taught that the world will know we are Christians by our love (13:35). I have never personally seen any Christian activist on an execution night misrepresent the name of Christ by violating these principles in His name. Angry and hateful protestors on either side represent their own selves. I respect the personal feelings and convictions of any Christian brother or sister— however they may feel about the issue. I am also proud of Christian activists for representing the name of Jesus with a good witness of dignity and respectful behavior. When the Church is represented by believers demonstrating love and self-control, they are showing that their dependence is on God—not an appellate judge or a governor.

During the highly emotional appeals and recounts of the 2000 presidential election, I was taught a valuable lesson about trusting God and praising Him no matter who might eventually be declared the winner of the election. From many sermons and commentaries during that period, I was reminded that God is in control, no matter which man became our president, and that our burdens should be carried to the church house, not to the White House. In the same way that we all have seen many completely different individuals in one congregation touched by the same sermon but in totally different and personal ways, I believe that God will somehow draw all believers closer to where He wants us to be regardless of where we stand on the issue of capital punishment.

I often observed that both sides of the execution controversy seem to be supported by some genuinely good and well-meaning people. Both sides have Christian advocates who feel they are representing an accurate Christian perspective of this moral dilemma. However, when determined to take a firm stand on any controversial issue, I learned that I could never claim to be representing the Christian view of the matter unless I had carefully considered two factors:

- *Is my stance or premise truly aligned with the Word of God?*
- *What is the true motive and condition of my heart?*

On the capital punishment issue, it could be very easy for me not to realize the true motive of my heart. My motive will ultimately be my foundation that will either support me or cause me to fall. I had to be absolutely clear about this: Is my stance founded on my own desires and personal agenda, or led by the Spirit of God?

Proverbs 21:2 tells us: "Every way of a man is right in his own eyes, but the LORD weighs the heart." Even a well-meaning Christian can become so bent on his or her own agenda that he or she forgets and contradicts the will of God. In the Sermon on the Mount, Jesus sternly warned us about distorting and perverting the heart of God's Law and His will in exchange for our own self-serving motives. If our predominant view of justice is determined by who we consider to be the most dangerous threat to our own personal agenda, then our foundation is of the world.

[X] Discerning the Truth

Once, when I was struggling to discern the truth over two sides of a controversy that were tugging my heart in opposite directions, the Holy Spirit led me to dwell upon James 4:1–4:

> *What causes quarrels and what causes fights among you? Is it not this, that your passions are at war within you? You desire and do not have, so you murder. You covet and cannot obtain, so you fight and quarrel. You do not have, because you do not ask. You ask and do not receive, because you ask wrongly, to spend it*

on your passions. You adulterous people! Do you not know that friendship with the world is enmity with God? Therefore whoever wishes to be a friend of the world makes himself an enemy of God.

The very idea of becoming an enemy of God was a bone-chilling thought, but I had to admit that one side of the controversy was pulling my heart in that direction.

- *If we want to reduce the powers of government and minimize their methods of accountability because they are restraining obstacles that limit our own self-interests, then we have chosen to make God our enemy.*

- *If we are seeking to have peace with the world at the cost of compromising the truth and tolerating evil, we are perverting the true peace Christ desires for us, and we have made God our enemy.*

- *If we value our physical lives in this world more than we value eternal life, then we have chosen to make God our enemy.*

- *If we are motivated by human comparison rather than Godly compassion, then we have chosen to make God our enemy.*

- *If we condemn the sinner more than the sin out of hate and vengeance, we make God our enemy.*

We must earnestly ask ourselves: "Where are our hearts?" Are they focused on God or on ourselves?

As I was reading what Jesus said in Matthew 5:6, "Blessed are those who hunger and thirst for righteousness" (or what is right), it occurred to me that both the anti–death penalty and pro–death penalty activists "appear" to be tremendously hungry and thirsty for what is right. If both opposing sides of a debate legitimately desire what is right but vehemently disagree on what is right, who settles the dispute?

When I took that question to my pastor, he told me that for Christians, God's will as described in God's Word settles the dispute of who is right. If we are prayerfully yearning for *God's* will to be done and

His grace to be shown in the midst of the oppression and injustice all around us, we are blessed. The Word tells us that people with a healthy, ravenous appetite for God's will to prevail will be filled with all spiritual blessings. If we are hungry and thirsty for *our own* will to be done, however, we are an obstacle and enemy to blessedness. This should be the guiding direction for our hungry hearts when discerning what is truly right. If it is not, we are in danger of following the nonbiblical worldview of justice.

I had to realize that the biblical definition of what is right seldom aligns with that of the world. Jesus told us, "If they persecuted Me, they will also persecute you" (John 15:20). This helped me realize that those certain activists who feared the Truth and appeared to hate me actually hated my Shepherd and His explanations of what is right. Majority opinion in elections can always shape and change the laws of humans, but it can never change the laws of God. In John 3:19, Jesus explains the reason that people are prone to reject and fight against His law.

The true answer to this dilemma does not lie with a government decision, determining current views of what is right. The only hope for justice is through God's standard of righteousness, not the government's. Time has proven that human standards are not standards at all but are constantly changing with the newest opinions of each new leader and each new generation. The Lord commands us to submit to the government (Romans 13:1–2) but to follow the standards He set for us in His Word.

I have three questions for every reader:

1. *Are you stubbornly holding a firm stance for or against the death penalty?*
2. *Are you also stubbornly holding on to the Word of God?*
3. *Which grip is tighter?*

God warned me repeatedly throughout the Bible not to turn to the left or to the right of His Word. If I became totally bent toward my own agenda, I would become bent too far right or too far left and way out of line with the Word of God. Both conservative and liberal Christians can wander away from the Truth if they do not hold unswervingly to the Word as their defining standard and direction. My long, grueling struggle between opposing perspectives of every dramatic dilemma came down to this deciding factor. If I really wanted to know and do God's will above my own, I had to study His Word and obey it. Being truly in the center of God's will rather than veering off to the left or to the right all became clear here. In the most challenging and emotional crises I faced, ignorance or confusion was no longer a factor, only obedience or disobedience (Isaiah 30:21).

When I was a lot younger, I did not need glasses, but I was blind to the Truth. When I did not know God or anything about His will, my grip was stubbornly holding on to my own self-interests. I was naïve, gullible prey for the merciless enemy to easily steal, kill, and destroy. A tree is known by its fruit, and a close examination of mine back then showed it was rotten because it revealed only a reflection of self. I thank God that by His grace, I survived the ignorance of my youth long enough to stop clinging to myself and start clinging to the Shepherd. When I finally learned to let God's Word determine the victor of the conflicts inside my heart, He changed my reflection in the mirror from mine to His. Growing to better represent Jesus as the image bearer He created me to be was a progressive blessing but also a progressive challenge. It led me to more confrontations with the unbelieving world (John 15:18–21). But if I had to have an enemy, I would much rather it be God's enemies than God Himself. I would much rather reflect Him than them. Therefore, after each confrontation with those embracing a nonbiblical worldview of justice, I simply cleaned my new glasses, adjusted them back on my face, and settled in with my Bible for a fresh reflection lesson.

CHAPTER 12

Shaped by Both Law and Gospel

Although I had become firmly resolved to stand on the foundation of God's Word as my guide for discerning right and wrong, I never liked to push the Bible down people's throats. That method didn't work because it only caused force-fed victims to regurgitate the truth. Instead, I tried hard to let my daily witness speak for itself. That method did work. It regularly prompted friends and co-workers to ask me if the Bible had anything to say about capital punishment. God opened many doors for me that way. When God gave people ears to hear the Gospel, they ingested the Word because they were hungry for it. That Word stayed inside them.

Because I distinctly remember how far away I was from God's will and His Word earlier in my career, I had a lot of respect for and patience with people who resembled my recent disposition. I had not forgotten that in the first few years after I began to read the Bible, my desire to be a daily witness for the Lord was a good intention but not always a reality. Because my spiritual growth was painfully slow and unbalanced, it took many years before I walked close enough with the Lord to cause people to ask me questions about Him and value my answer. My efforts to properly reflect the image of the Shepherd while working in prison were a never-ending struggle that required constant prayer and meditation on God's Word.

Being mindful of where I came from was a blessing for me. My thoughts about justice and mercy had completely changed from when I started my criminal justice career journey. As I traveled the path of learning God's will through His Word, I distinctly remember being confident about my progress toward exhibiting the appropriate attitude and behavior of a sheep of God's flock until the day I was assigned to the death squad. The one thing I remember most about that day was how my confidence in that regard was suddenly shaken, causing my heart and soul to whirl into an instant spiritual crisis.

When I was first placed on the death squad, I felt so out of place. My passion was to help save and restore lives, but my job seemed to be an instrument to destroy lives. My heart's desire was to please God and do what was in the best interest of His people. So I had to face the following questions head-on: Was capital punishment really in the best interest of His people? Could this ever actually be in the best interest of the condemned? Could I please God and represent Him properly while serving the state on the death squad?

Although I struggled with many questions to which I did not have the answers, I knew where to find them. Whenever I diligently sought the Lord's counsel, He was always faithful to give me direction and understanding. Therefore, I confidently devoted myself to the deepest prayer and most exhaustive Bible study possible.

I had done a similar thing many years earlier when I was made a prison disciplinary hearing officer, presiding daily over inmate court cases dealing with laws and rules violated within the prison. I quickly became uncomfortable with the realization of how much power I was exercising over so many inmates' lives. My daily rulings were seemingly destroying these men's very lives.

The sentences that I would pass down on a daily basis kept men in prison for years longer than they would have otherwise served. My decisions routinely resulted in their living conditions within the prison being reduced to extreme discomfort and hardship. I understood that my role as a disciplinary judge was indeed a heavy responsibility under God. Eventually, through a lot of prayer and Bible reading, I resolved that these men were certainly a lot better off being judged by a God-fearing Christian than otherwise. I understood that I also had a

Judge to whom I was constantly accountable, and this kept me before Him in constant prayer for wisdom and discernment.

☒ Focusing on God's Word

By that point in my journey of spiritual development, I had already resolved that God's Word would be my absolute guide for discerning right from wrong. Being an inmate disciplinary hearing judge was indeed uncomfortable, but being appointed to the death squad was an even heavier discomfort. I could deal with discomfort, but I could never have accepted the appointment if I had discovered that allowing the government to have the power to wield the sword was against God's will.

My resolve drove me to search through numerous Christian bookstores for publications that offered biblical counsel on the subject of capital punishment. Much to my discouragement, I found a tremendous void of information on the subject. I was told this was because there were some disagreements within a couple of Christian denominations concerning the death penalty, which caused many publishers to have discomfort in dealing with such a controversial subject.

I wanted to find and investigate the feelings of any Christians who were against the death penalty. I searched until I found a few churches that were against the death penalty, and I read some of their publications on the subject. Their books took a strong stand against capital punishment; however, they were either not at all biblically based or they were extremely out of balance with parts of Scripture, leaving out any comments of Law and only mentioning mercy.

Back when I was first counseled by Dr. Beto to let the grace of the Gospel speak to me and not just the Law, I started doing so and have made progress at that ever since. The more I grew in recognizing their critically important value, the more I realized that I had been focused only on Law and intentionally ignoring the Lord's correlating, nearby Scriptures on grace and mercy. The Christian anti–death penalty books I read, however, were doing the exact opposite by intentionally ignoring the Lord's Law. The authors used their personal opinions about social and political concerns to formulate a well-sounding but completely unbiblical basis for their arguments.

They were insinuating that the Old Testament was Law and the New Testament was Gospel and that the two were not compatible. The truth, however, is that both have Law and Gospel. The Old Testament serves the New Testament and the New Testament gives meaning to and complements the Old Testament. They are both the Word of God and have the same author with the same continuous revelation of His message. The Law serves the Gospel and the Gospel is served by the Law. The Old Testament is actually all about Jesus (Luke 24:27).

These authors whose message was all mercy and no Law reminded me of the apostle Peter's well-sounding argument and personal feelings that prompted Jesus to tell him, "You are not setting your mind on the things of God, but on the things of man" (Mark 8:33). Jesus knew that Satan, the leader of human wolves, was speaking through Peter and causing him to think in ways opposed to God's will. The world presents many options and choices for how to view or consider the death penalty. Our personal feelings can cause us to be led into adopting a dangerous and nonbiblical position on this subject. Eventually, we can be like Peter and feel so strongly about something that our zealous feelings cloud our ability to recognize and accept the truth.

To avoid an out-of-balance view from either perspective, I took the authors' mentions of mercy that they used to justify their fight against the death penalty and found that in every one of them, the Lord had provided a connection to Law that they had intentionally ignored. Below are the mercy passages I found in their publications.

Romans 6:14–15 — We are not under Law but under grace.
Luke 6:29 — Jesus teaches us to "turn the other cheek" to those who wrong us.

Romans 12:17—We are warned not to repay injury with injury.

Acts 7:60—Stephen asks God to forgive those who are murdering him.

Matthew 5:44—Jesus tells us to love our enemies.

Matthew 18:15–35—Jesus tells us to love our brother who sins against us.

Philippians 2:3   We should always consider others better than ourselves.

Luke 23:34—Jesus asks His Father to forgive those who are murdering him.

Luke 6:41—Jesus tells us not to take the splinter out of our brother's eye but the beam out of our own.

Every one of these passages is certainly true and critically important, but each is twisted out of context when we intentionally ignore the connected reference to Law. Sobering verses of God's wrath are always connected to comforting verses of His grace and mercy. Likewise, God's counsel for mercy is always connected to His restraining warnings of Law.

Law and Gospel are two sides of the same goal of the Word of God. Redemption and wrath are two sides of the same coin. The intended goal of God's wrath is to result in repentance and restoration. Wrath serves mercy. When we look at Scripture through a proper balance of Law and Gospel, we are able to see ourselves in the story as God desires—not as we desire. The intended goal of mercy is faith and hope. Mercy is served by wrath.

- *When God's Law is a curb, used to set boundaries for restraining evil in society, this protection of God's sheep from predatory wolves is Law that is also grace. It is justice that is also mercy.*

- *When God's Law is a mirror, it enables us to see ourselves as sinners needing forgiveness. This understanding drives us to Christ in a humble posture of repentance, which receives grace. This is Law that is also mercy.*

- *When God's Law is a guide, it shows us how to please God, and we desire to follow His commandments in order to live respectfully of God and neighbor. This is Law that is also mercy concerning our relationship with God and one another.*

Seeking first the kingdom of God requires seeking His will through His balance of Law and Gospel. I believed the words of Proverbs 3:5–6: "Trust in the LORD with all your heart, and do not lean on your own understanding. In all your ways acknowledge Him, and He will make straight your paths." Because I persisted in seeking first the kingdom of God and His righteousness, and would not be swayed by secular views on this subject, the Lord helped me find many more examples of balanced Law and Gospel scriptural counsel than in this chapter. Out of the storms of conflicting influences and emotional struggle, I surrendered to accept and follow the biblical guidance about government executions. Although there were some serious heart issues I had to learn, the Lord guided me to know that I could obediently serve Him in all areas where He was at work in and around the capital punishment spectrum.

I was totally dependent upon the biblical revelations God showed me in that part of my journey, which made the rest of my journey possible. I clearly understood that the core foundation of all biblical counsel comes from what Jesus called the greatest and most important commandment, recorded in Matthew 22:37–39. We are to "love the Lord [our] God with all [our] heart and with all [our] soul and with all [our] mind . . . and love [our] neighbor as [ourselves]." Jesus told us that all of God's Law and all of His biblical counsel are centered in these two commands. The atoning blood of Christ is our ultimate example of this type of love.

I was shown that if I am a true follower of Jesus, this commandment should guide every decision in my life. In the same way that all legal disputes in America are weighed against the US Constitution, and all who claim citizenship or residence here must submit themselves to the guidelines in that law; all who pledge allegiance to

Christ must place themselves under the governing law that He called the most important.

I understood that the greatest commandment was given to all believers to guide every aspect of our personal lives. The Shepherd commands each individual sheep to be loving, compassionate, merciful, and forgiving, even to the most vicious wolves who hate and kill us. This is the mind of Christ. What the greatest commandment teaches is *personal* humility and *individual* self-temperance of our hearts when dealing with our fellow man.

What I did not understand was that this commandment is not to be confused with God's equally clear guidance and instruction on the *role of government* in matters of maintaining social order and justice. These guidelines for individuals and governments are not the same. God is passionate about both justice and mercy. Jesus called justice and mercy the more important matters of the Law (Matthew 23:23). The two complement each other, and Christians can pursue both without contradiction.

The Lord helped me realize that it is a perversion of the truth to hold exclusively to grace and mercy while rejecting God's Law and His justice. Without God's Law and justice, there is no sin, and therefore no need for a Savior or His Gospel. Jesus is both the Lion and the Lamb. He is the Lamb of grace, mercy, and gentle, loving compassion, but He is also the Lion of truth, power, and justice. The perfect balance of the Lion and the Lamb in Jesus Christ is the perfect model of character for us to imitate. I must love wolves with compassion, mercy, and ministry, but I must also hold them and myself accountable in submission to the restraints and consequences set forth in God's Law and His justice.

[X] Matters of the Heart

The Lord showed me that both justice and mercy are matters of the heart. Our hearts must yearn to live as Jesus lived (1 John 2:6).

To do this, we must have a heart of mercy and ministry toward others while allowing the government to be and do what God has ordained it to do. Jesus never resisted or rebelled against the Roman government; rather, He instructed us to submit to governmental authority. The following are but a few examples in the New Testament where God empowered and ordained the government to rule over us and enforce punishment against us when we do wrong:

> *Be subject for the Lord's sake to every human institution, whether it be to the emperor as supreme, or to governors as sent by him to punish those who do evil and to praise those who do good. (1 Peter 2:13–14)*

> *Let every person be subject to the governing authorities. For there is no authority except from God, and those that exist have been instituted by God. Therefore whoever resists the authorities resists what God has appointed, and those who resist will incur judgment. For rulers are not a terror to good conduct, but to bad. Would you have no fear of the one who is in authority? Then do what is good, and you will receive his approval, for he is God's servant for your good. But if you do wrong, be afraid, for he does not bear the sword in vain. For he is the servant of God, an avenger who carries out God's wrath on the wrongdoer. (Romans 13:1–4)*

> *Remind them to be submissive to rulers and authorities, to be obedient, to be ready for every good work. (Titus 3:1)*

The Old Testament is filled with justifications for capital punishment, but the New Testament gives the same direction. The Scripture verses above are clear New Testament biblical counsel that God not only allows governments to use the sword (capital punishment), but ordains them to do so. God allows human governments to use force against us to provide order and protect us from evil.

When studying God's actions to restrain evil on our behalf, I became acquainted with His wrath. Consistent with the Great Commandment is Jesus' teaching to "seek first the kingdom of God and His righteousness" (Matthew 6:33). God's righteousness necessarily includes His justice. I have been on both sides of this thinking. I once thought only about punitive justice and legalistic righteousness. I have also thought like so many other Christians who wanted to focus solely on God's unconditional love and mercy and intentionally choose to overlook His warnings of wrath. It was eye-opening for me to discover that our Lord's love and His wrath are both reflected in His righteous judgment. We need to know the truth about God's love and mercy, but we also must know the truth about God's wrath. To embrace either one without the other would be a deceptive and unhealthy imbalance.

The Shepherd makes it very clear that His sheep are to love the wolves who prey upon them, but they are also to love His Law (Psalm 119:97), which keeps us from sin (Psalm 119:11) and provides consequences for all who choose to live by the sword of violence.

Submitting to God's methods of justice does not mean that Christian crime fighters and justice workers don't love murderers; rather, it means that we love God more than we love our own lives. Jesus warned us that if we loved our lives, we would lose them (John 12:25). We must indeed love the sinner, but not be deceived and lured into compromising the counsel and Law of God on dealing with the sin. The Bible does not teach us that God's love and mercy means to condone, ignore, and tolerate crime and sin; rather, it teaches that love is shown through discipline (Proverbs 13:24).

As a disciplinary hearing officer, I quickly learned that whenever I ignored injustice, it only got worse. I used to think that I was practicing "godly lenience" when I occasionally let an inmate get away with little or no consequences for his crimes in prison. On every one of those occasions, I later realized that I was actually being used by Satan to lure that inmate into a deeper comfort level with his criminal and sinful behavior, and the resulting consequences were always catastrophic.

X Tolerance of Evil

I learned the hard way that one of the deadliest causes of the infectious spread of evil was my "tolerance" of evil. When I ignored, tolerated, or condoned the defiance of man's laws or God's laws, I was ignoring biblical counsel and substituting my own personal opinion in place of God's standard of justice.

When the Lord showed me those truths, He was quick to make sure that I did not develop a condemning heart. He showed me that if I became personally judgmental or took vengeance into my own hands, I would not be following God's standard of justice either (Romans 12:17). Leaving vengeance to God and supporting His appointed methods of dealing with those who live by the sword of violence is His true standard of justice (Romans 12:19). When I understood and lived by this biblical balance of justice and mercy, by serving the state I was not taking God's place but properly serving God according to His purpose.

The Lord drove this lesson deeper into my heart when I studied the account of His confrontation with the woman caught in adultery (John 8:1–11). At first glance I mistakenly thought that Jesus was pardoning a death sentence. When I examined some commentaries, however, I considered how Jesus confronted her accusers before He confronted the woman. He peeled away their pretended concern for God's Law and exposed the fact that their own sinful condition was even more heinous than hers. Jesus showed them that they were facing greater judgment without mercy because of their own hearts of condemnation (James 2:13). As their hearts felt the conviction of their individual guilt, they departed one by one.

Jesus did not teach a tolerance of evil, nor was He excusing the woman's sin. He was demonstrating the perfect balance of justice and mercy. Our Lord condemned the hearts of vengeance and self-righteousness in her accusers while compassionately but definitely condemning the sin of the adulterous woman. No one is more compassionate to sinners than Jesus! However, no one is more severely against sin than He!

I discovered that the truth is always divisive, and any time I stand for the truth, not everyone will agree with me. Those who disagree with biblical counsel see things from their own personal perspective, which has been shaped by painful experiences or close influential acquaintances, but not necessarily by the truth of God's Word. I respect the opinions and feelings of others, but I must align myself with the truth. If I had listened to all the advice and opinions I received concerning my job, I would have been far from aligned with the truth. Virtually all criticism came from those who had none or only half of the truth.

It is indeed good, sound Christian teaching to hold high the sanctity of life and to be disturbed at the taking of a human life by any means, but preserving a human life does not come before the preservation of the truth. I personally knew some believers who had become anti–death penalty activists based on sanctity of life concepts that were politically correct, but not at all biblically correct. I learned that believers who have accidentally and innocently embraced an errant premise as an absolute Christian moral standard are well-meaning brothers and sisters, but they desperately need to be gently and lovingly enlightened with the "complete" truth.

I once heard a man criticize some fellow Christians as hypocrites because they supported capital punishment yet were against abortion.

He felt that both were the same. He did not understand that the Bible guides Christians to honor the sanctity of life by honoring and submitting to the methods of law enforcement and control that God has instituted to protect His sheep from wolves. Both capital punishment and anti-abortion efforts protect innocent people from murder. The complete truth of the Bible explains that God wants us as individuals to have a heart of mercy while also having a heart that honors and respects His justice.

☒ The Sword of the State

I have occasionally been hammered with the question, "Don't you feel guilty for assisting in the executions of all of those men and women?" I never answer that question with explanations of how God allows and ordains capital punishment unless I also have the opportunity to fully explain the difference between God's counsel for individual self-temperance and His counsel for governments. Giving only half of that explanation would only set people up to feel self-righteous and judgmental about how horrible some criminal was, how despicable the crime was, and how that person needed and deserved to die.

If I only explained half of the truth, I would be helping people to be exactly like the Pharisees who wanted to stone the adulterous woman. They were looking for ways to elevate their own righteousness by putting others beneath them and hating them. Thankfully, the Lord usually arranges for me to have enough time to explain the whole truth that as individuals, we must not judge others or we will be just as guilty as the person we want to condemn and hate.

God did not give the power of the sword to me as an individual or to the Church, but He did give it to the government and appointed me as His servant in the government. Therefore, biblical direction for the Christian attitude toward capital punishment would be to have a heart of ministry and compassion for the murderous wolf while cooperating with the government's methods of dealing with the crime.

When King Solomon asked for wisdom and discernment to properly govern God's people, he received that ability but also struggled with personal feelings that often led him away from God's will. In his ability to discern God's justice, he wrote:

> *For everything there is a season, and a time for every matter under heaven: a time to be born, and a time to die; a time to plant, and a time to pluck up what is planted; a time to kill, and a time to heal. (Ecclesiastes 3:1–3)*

The red-letter words of Christ Himself taught me His mercy as well as His justice. In the parable of the wedding banquet, Jesus tells of how He will have great patience and mercy as He tries to gather His wayward sheep, but we eventually force Him to discipline us in righteous judgment:

> *But they paid no attention and went off, one to his farm, another to his business, while the rest seized his servants, treated them shamefully, and killed them. The king was angry, and he sent his troops and destroyed those murderers and burned their city. (Matthew 22:5–7)*

When I first read this I wondered, Who is this army that God sends? Then I learned that it is the earthly government He has empowered to protect us and to further His plans for His kingdom. When we see the innocent being victimized, Christ teaches us to leave all vengeance to our heavenly King while recognizing the army He raises up as His instruments of justice. Although Jesus taught me several different lessons from this parable, certainly one of them was to understand the character of justice in the heart of the King. God's great and jealous love for His faithful servants eventually moves Him to discipline the wolves who mercilessly prey upon them.

The Lord showed me another example of His mercy and justice in Luke 13:6–9:

> He told this parable: "A man had a fig tree planted in his vineyard, and he came seeking fruit on it and found none. And he said to the vinedresser, 'Look, for three years now I have come seeking fruit on this fig tree, and I find none. Cut it down. Why should it use up the ground?' And he answered him, 'Sir, let it alone this year also, until I dig around it and put on manure. Then if it should bear fruit next year, well and good; but if not, you can cut it down.'"

The ability of our Lord to forgive and save us is absolutely unlimited, but His love calls for Him to correct us as needed according to His infinite wisdom and justice.

When Jesus was questioned about God's mercy and protection from suffering or government oppression, He warned the people to consider their own behavior or the same thing could happen to them:

> There were some present at that very time who told Him about the Galileans whose blood Pilate had mingled with their sacrifices. And He answered them, "Do you think that these Galileans were worse sinners than all the other Galileans, because they suffered in this way? No, I tell you; but unless you repent, you will all likewise perish. Or those eighteen on whom the tower in Siloam fell and killed them: do you think that they were worse offenders than all

the others who lived in Jerusalem? No, I tell you; but
unless you repent, you will all likewise perish." (Luke
13:1–5)

It was clear to me that God is a God of salvation, mercy, and compassion who desires that all people live abundant and fruitful lives.
It also became clear, however, that since the first death sentence on
Adam, we all must reap the wages and consequences of our sins here
on earth even though we can be forgiven and saved eternally. There
are consequences to actions. Jesus did not do away with temporal consequences to actions. He did away with eternal consequences.

Jesus told the thief on the cross, "Today you will be with Me in
Paradise" (Luke 23:43). In this divine declaration of pardon, Jesus did
not save the thief's physical life; He saved his eternal life. Jesus let the
thief continue to suffer through his execution and pay the temporal
consequences for his crimes. This is a clear example of how God's
mercy and justice are always in perfect harmony and are never a contradiction.

Both the Old Testament and the New Testament give God's
promises on two basic fundamental truths of His mercy and justice:

1. *When we repent of our sin and turn to God, we can expect*
    eternal pardon and forgiveness (1 John 1:9; 2 Chronicles
    7:14).

2. *When we turn away from God in rebellious disobedience,*
    we can expect temporal (earthly) consequences because
    of His love (Romans 2:8, Hosea 8:7; and Deuteronomy
    28:15–68).

The Bible occasionally refers to Satan and his followers as "the
lawless ones." If we ignored God's provisions for the restraint of evil,
then lawlessness would reign. We would be easy prey if God had not
arranged for governing authorities and their threatened use of force.
God has given our earthly governments the power to maintain public order and peace, including the power to take up arms to execute

governmental vengeance against enemies of peace and order. God's provision of governmental authorities, especially the force they use to protect order and promote good, make our life together as peaceful citizens possible.

A Scripture passage that has been well used for this point by some, but occasionally perverted out of context by others, is Matthew 5:38–40, where Jesus says:

> You have heard that it was said, "An eye for an eye and a tooth for a tooth." But I say to you, Do not resist the one who is evil. But if anyone slaps you on the right cheek, turn to him the other also. And if anyone would sue you and take your tunic, let him have your cloak as well.

The Lord is not instructing us to let crime go unpunished. He is certainly not telling us that if someone rapes and murders our wife, we should give him our daughter as well. (Don't laugh, there are some who have believed and taught this.) What Jesus is actually telling us is that as individuals, we must not have a heart of vengeance or kill for personal motives.

King David provides one of the clearest biblical examples for the understanding of God's will in this matter. When David was motivated to have one man killed strictly for personal reasons, he displeased God. When David killed tens of thousands of people as a warrior, however, he pleased God. God was with this mighty warrior and even referred to him as a man after His own heart.

Genesis 9:6 provides another command from the Lord that exemplifies government-ordained authority to wield the sword to protect the sheep from the wolves: "Whoever sheds the blood of man, by man shall his blood be shed, for God made man in His own image." In this passage, God instructs that "by man" a murderer's life must be taken, because murder is an assault on the image of God.

Some translate the Fifth Commandment in Exodus 20:13 as "You shall not kill," but the correct translation of the Hebrew verb *ratsah* is "murder." This is verified by God's immediate counsel in the following chapter (Exodus 21:12–14) on dealing with those who break this commandment. In this holiness code, God doesn't only "allow" capital punishment of murderers, He commands it. This explanation of the Commandments clarifies the meaning of God's command no matter which word is used in the translation.

The Holy Scriptures show that God will indeed turn us over to His appointed "agents of wrath" when we mock His mercy and choose to live by the sword.

> *Jesus said to him, " . . . all who take the sword will perish by the sword." (Matthew 26:52)*

> *Though they know God's righteous decree that those who practice such things deserve to die, they not only do them but give approval to those who practice them. (Romans 1:32)*

> *Do not be deceived: God is not mocked, for whatever one sows, that will he also reap. (Galatians 6:7)*

> *But as for these enemies of mine, who did not want me to reign over them, bring them here and slaughter them before me. (Luke 19:27)*

> *The wrongdoer will be paid back for the wrong he has done, and there is no partiality. (Colossians 3:25)*

*If anyone is to be taken captive, to captivity he goes;
if anyone is to be slain with the sword, with the sword
must he be slain. Here is a call for the endurance and
faith of the saints. (Revelation 13:10)*

*Do you not know that you are God's temple and that
God's Spirit dwells in you? If anyone destroys God's
temple, God will destroy him. For God's temple is holy,
and you are that temple. (1 Corinthians 3:16–17)*

*For if God did not spare angels when they sinned
. . . if He did not spare the ancient world . . . when
He brought a flood upon the world of the ungodly;
if by turning the cities of Sodom and Gomorrah to
ashes He condemned them to extinction, making
them an example of what is going to happen to the
ungodly; . . . then the Lord knows how to rescue the
godly from trials, and to keep the unrighteous under
punishment until the day of judgment, and especially
those who indulge in the lust of defiling passion and
despise authority. . . . These, like irrational animals,
creatures of instinct, born to be caught and destroyed,
blaspheming about matters of which they are
ignorant, will also be destroyed in their destruction,
suffering wrong as the wage for their wrongdoing.
(2 Peter 2:4a, 5–6, 9–10a, 12–13a)*

Or do you presume on the riches of His kindness and forbearance and patience, not knowing that God's kindness is meant to lead you to repentance? But because of your hard and impenitent heart you are storing up wrath for yourself on the day of wrath when God's righteous judgment will be revealed. He will render to each one according to his works: to those who by patience in well-doing seek for glory and honor and immortality, He will give eternal life; but for those who are self-seeking and do not obey the truth, but obey unrighteousness, there will be wrath and fury. (Romans 2:4–8)

If then I am a wrongdoer and have committed anything for which I deserve to die, I do not seek to escape death. (Acts 25:11a)

One of the most challenging questions from anti–death penalty Christians is, "Would Jesus ever execute someone?" When Jesus physically lived His life on earth, His life taught us how to live as individuals. As individuals, we are not supposed to execute anyone. Therefore, consistent with the truth, Jesus would not ever have executed anyone. Jesus did, however, live a life that certainly recognized, respected, and honored the government's authority to execute people. God did not give the power of the sword of justice to individuals, but to the state.

As some of you consider these truths for the first time, I pray you do not make the mistake of thinking that God is harsh, vindictive, and mean. The truth is that all of this simply shows just how loving and merciful God is! He doesn't want anyone to choose a path that leads to death by execution, but He loves us enough to give us the ability to choose it. Actually, the truth is that we are all sentenced to death—

with the exact same sentence as Adam. In God's great love and mercy, however, He allows us to make lifestyle choices that can contribute heavily to the manner in which that death will occur.

When any of us are called by our government to serve on a jury in a capital murder trial, we do not have to feel like we are in a moral dilemma by participating in delivering a verdict or a sentence. If the evidence compelling a juror to make a decision of guilt is beyond all shadow of a doubt, then voting any other way would be against God's will. In the punishment phase of the trial, choosing between a sentence of life without parole or a sentence of death is not a choice between right and wrong. The juror has been delegated and ordained by God to pass judgment not as a private individual, but as a servant of God and the government; therefore either choice is biblically justified and in line with God's will. (Exodus 21:12–14 gives exceptions to a capital punishment penalty for mitigating circumstances.)

On the other hand, if a juror performs this duty with a heart of personal hate and prejudice, this is against biblical counsel (Exodus 23:1–3, 6–8) and is out of line with God's will. When serving on a sentencing jury, to choose between hating a murderous wolf with a vengeance because of his or her actions or loving that person with compassion is a choice between right and wrong. Christians can definitely serve as a juror in any type of trial as long as they are not biased or prejudiced in their hearts. In fact, the ideal jury for achieving true justice would be one that is full of Christians who fear God and desire His will above their own.

Though some controversial issues tugged my heart in different directions, I became resilient to those with a nonbiblical worldview that rejected God's will to give the power of the sword to the state. These opponents could not understand how a loving, merciful God could ever allow suffering or permit painful consequences for wrong decisions. They had succumbed to the same temptation I had felt, but they chose to follow their emotions away from the Lord until they became entrenched far to the left of God's counsel in His Word.

Their stance to promote unbridled mercy was actually a tool of defiant rebellion against the sovereignty of God. Just as Jonah hated his enemies more than he loved God, some sheep of God's pasture can hate capital punishment more than they love God. Mercy motivated by self-interest with no regard for God's will is a perversion of mercy and a recipe for catastrophe. This response to a perceived evil is worse than the evil they have imagined.

Christian readers, do not allow this issue of capital punishment to be an instrument of division and separation between you and your brothers or sisters in Christ. If Satan hasn't caused enough grief through successfully tempting someone to commit capital murder, he will use this subject of capital punishment to sow bitterness and discord among the Church. I implore you not to be a pawn in that game. Blessedness does not come from opposing or embracing capital punishment, but rather from embracing Jesus Christ. If we reverently and respectfully fear the Lord and truly find delight in His commands, we will look to the Shepherd and be guided in the right direction.

I depended upon God's guidance constantly so that He could use me to touch others each day. I didn't need to dwell on exactly how He might use me each moment; rather I just needed to commit my thoughts and actions to obeying, serving, and pleasing Him.

- *Sometimes I was called to be an agent of His mercy.*
- *Sometimes I was called to be an agent of His wrath.*
- *Many times I was called to be both.*
- *All of the time I was crying out to God for His help to be His instrument to do His will for His people.*

I was appointed and commissioned as a government authority to help carry out the sad and unfortunate task of dealing with wolves who lived by the sword of violence. I know that God intentionally placed me in that position to be used by Him as a light in a dark situation. I was able to be that light as long as I properly discerned the truth in justice against a barrage of multifaceted opinions of humans. I always found that truth in God's Word and in constant prayer. I imitated the prayer of young King Solomon, who asked God for the wisdom to know what to do. I imitated the prayer of King Jehoshaphat in crying out to God in complete dependence, admitting that I was powerless in this dilemma and did not know what to do . . . but my eyes were on Him! Daily, I got down on my knees and looked to the Shepherd for help and guidance. Then I got up off of my knees and served Him as I was led.

CHAPTER 13

Shaped by Serving in Two Kingdoms

My eyes squinted in reaction to the bright sunlight as I walked out of the dark prison, through the big iron entrance gates, and out onto the front porch of the Walls Unit. I stood there for a while, looking around at the different participants in the execution night activities. To my left, at the end of the street, was a very small, calm gathering of protestors. Just to the right of that little crowd were the media teams whose numbers were also minimal. Straight ahead of me were the state police—in their positions, but relaxed because of the nonthreatening atmosphere. I was thankful for the docile tone of the evening, because many times I had stood on that porch and experienced extremely different sights, sounds, and attitudes. I had endured many verbal assaults from inmates inside the prison, but I experienced as many or more from protestors on the outside as I stood on that porch.

As I looked to my far right, my attention was captured by a fascinating sight. It was a prison guard. He was a seasoned veteran correctional officer working the number 1 gun tower. The stern-faced prison guard took his job very seriously. He was professionally dressed in a crisp, clean, starched, and pressed uniform. His black boots were polished to a high shine. His hair was trimmed to regulation length and perfectly groomed. He was a middle-aged man but kept himself in lean, disciplined physical shape. He was standing perfectly erect as he moved his eyes slowly from left to right. The rifle in his hands was being held with a tight grip and placed close to his chest. He had chosen a position out on the catwalk (the balcony surrounding the

A gun tower officer vigilantly watches one section of the massive wall surrounding the Walls Unit.

gun tower) that gave him the best possible view from his post high on top of the northwest perimeter wall.

He was so attentive to watching the wall that he had not yet noticed that I was watching him from the front porch of the prison. Within a few minutes, however, he took a quick walk around the entire catwalk to be sure of his complete surroundings. As he was scoping out the area, he saw me looking up at him. He gave me a silent head nod of recognition, and I quietly nodded back in affirmation. Then, once again, his eyes were scanning the perimeter. As I gazed at this guard on his post, I had tremendous respect and appreciation for the committed service he displayed.

While I was watching him, my mind raced back to the time I used to perform that same duty. I knew very well how difficult it was to remain ultimately vigilant, looking at the same section of a perimeter for eight hours straight. I remembered how easy it was to accidentally allow some commotion or amusing distraction to take my concentration from the perimeter, creating a potentially dangerous vulnerability. Sometimes those distractions are an intentionally planned diversion to give an inmate an opportunity to escape or for someone to throw contraband over the wall and into the compound. Control of a prison can break down in only one moment of negligence.

As I reminisced about those early days in my career, a peculiar awareness came over me. I can remember standing there, thinking: "It's now two decades later, and I'm still here. I'm still serving the state of Texas, still serving inmates, still serving their surviving victims, still serving God in this crazy place."

Then I remember thinking: "Yes, I'm still here, but what a huge difference from twenty years ago." Back in those earliest days, I never considered myself to be serving God or anyone but myself. I did not yet follow the Lord and I was only there for the paycheck. The way I felt about human wolves back then was entirely different, because my heart was different. From the moment I was given ears to hear the Gospel, the desire of my heart instantly changed, but the actual condition of my heart struggled to grow and develop over my entire career. I was still working in a place of darkness, but my ability to navigate through it grew stronger as I learned the value of retaining each lesson the Lord taught me along the way.

I snapped out of my reminiscing mode and stepped off the porch to walk across the street. It was time to pat search the families and bring them in to witness the execution. It was a quiet, peaceful evening, but it was extremely emotional for me because this execution would be my last.

⟦X⟧ Church and State

One lesson I had learned from the Lord was to trust Him when it appeared that He wanted me to make a move. Each promotion to a new position and each prison unit change in my career required faith and trust, but I was convinced that each move was His will.

When I became convinced that His will for me to serve Him on the death squad was drawing to an end, I began to make plans for my retirement. I had served in two "kingdoms" by His will for the right duration, and the time had come to give greater priority to a different direction outside of the prison.

I learned in one of my pastor's Bible studies that any Christian whose vocation is to serve the government has answered a good calling of critical importance, but our service and positions are all part of an earthly kingdom with temporal authority. Christians who serve the government are also required to serve a spiritual authority. Both authorities are actually two different kingdoms or two governments that God has established. These two authorities are church and state.

We have a responsibility to serve both kingdoms simultaneously but should always distinguish a priority service to the kingdom of God. This is not to be confused with the difference between God's kingdom and the "kingdom" of Satan, but is rather the difference between civil and spiritual authorities established by God out of concern for His people.

With the understanding that I had responsibly fulfilled my duties to the state for over two decades and with a lot of prayer and answered prayer, I was able to feel right about putting my life of service to the temporal kingdom behind me.

☒ Moving On

It seemed a little ironic that I had once struggled to reconcile my calling to work in the execution profession. Now I was struggling to reconcile my calling to leave it. Most of my adult life, my education and my professional experience had been invested in serving the state of Texas in this criminal justice career. I had poured my heart into serving God and His people in this position, so unplugging my heart from this duty was very difficult.

God gave me a couple of helpful motivations to make the decision a little easier. One prompting was that my wife, Jill, was appointed to a position with a powerful ministry at a church over fifty miles from Huntsville. She had been commuting over an hour each way every day for a couple years. Her fit in that ministry team was such a huge blessing to her and them that her service to the kingdom of God deserved my total priority support.

A secondary motivation for retiring and moving were my thoughts about enrolling in a theological seminary to start a second career serving the Lord in some form of full-time ministry. I decided that these moves would be necessary steps in that direction. I had no specific plans for any ministry direction, only a determination to follow a yearning I felt in my heart to serve the Lord much more than I had been able to up to that point.

As I was winding down my final few months of state employment, I no longer felt that I was leaving it all behind. Instead, I felt like I was taking all of the amazing life lessons from death row that God enabled me to learn in order to use them in some form of ministry. The journey of experiences God used to teach the lessons had been brutal, but by His grace I had survived—except for the parts of me that needed to die.

Even in the last weeks before my retirement, the Lord was still teaching—still shaping me. My pastor's teachings about serving two different kingdoms led me to learn three similar but separate lessons down the home stretch of my career. Each separate lesson had to do with distractions from keeping the condition of my heart aligned with God's kingdom agenda.

☒ Who Controls Your Heart?

The Lord taught me that He is either pleased or displeased with His sheep based on the condition of our hearts. One of the most important messages I would be taking with me to share outside the prison was that even the most well-meaning sheep of God's pasture can make choices that are seriously displeasing to Him if our hearts are not aligned with His. Whether we are serving the state or serving God and His Church, having our priorities right actually boils down to whom we allow to control our hearts.

Whenever I chose to serve an earthly government agenda more devotedly than I served God and His Church, my heart was more aligned with the enemy's than with God's, and I was upside down in my priorities of serving in two kingdoms.

Watching that gun-tower guard avoid distractions and thinking back to my similar experiences, I realized that many times, the things that caused me to serve the earthy kingdom with more devotion were intentional distractions from the enemy to divert my focus away from God and leave my heart completely vulnerable for derailment. While God was trying to mold and shape me for His purposes, Satan was always trying to do the same.

Therefore, the first antidistraction strategy I employed was a *specific personal prayer*. I asked for

- *clarity of hearing, that I might clearly recognize the voice of the Shepherd above all other voices competing for my attention;*
- *clarity of thinking, that I might make decisions that are more pleasing to God than pleasing to any others I serve; and*
- *clarity of memory, that I might never forget that God is ultimately in control and will honor my seeking Him first.*

The battle for the convictions of my heart and which kingdom I would be most loyal to raged every day. My gun-tower reflections triggered memories of the condition of my heart when I served the earthly kingdom with more zeal and did not seek first the kingdom of God.

Even after receiving God's grace, I was resistant to give grace. With my heart in that condition, it was easy to hate wolves and difficult to love them. We are warned in 1 John 3:15 that whoever hates a brother is no different than a murderer. From that perspective, wolves may have slain thousands, but self-righteous sheep have slain tens of thousands. When I took my righteous indignation too far to the right, it become hate, and my response to evil could have been worse than the evil itself. Mine was a misdirected priority focus and an abuse of God's ordained governmental authority.

God drove this lesson deep into my heart through an inmate whom we will call Craig. His crime was killing five men at once in a quick, thirty-second burst of anger. Craig was a wolf, but he was a wise old man, and I enjoyed listening to him talk. On one such occasion, he told me deer-hunting stories. He described how bucks have great survival instincts that serve them well out in the wild. He said, "They are so wise and elusive that humans seldom ever even catch a quick glimpse of them." Then he smiled and said, "But there is a certain, short period of time each year in the fall called 'the rut,' when bucks temporarily lose their survival instincts that have kept them alive and healthy. During this little span of time, their complete focus is on mating. This distraction from what they know full well is necessary for sustaining their lives often results in their death. They suddenly become easy prey for hunters."

At this point in his story, Craig paused and dropped his head. Then he looked up at me and said, "You know, I guess that's kind of what happened to me. Those guys I killed had messed me over really bad. I was so focused on revenge, that I was completely distracted from my knowledge of right and wrong."

As I listened to him, I could feel the Holy Spirit telling me that the enemy of our souls is hunting each of us, and we become easy prey for him when we get distracted from the truth. This inmate's response to evil was certainly worse than the evil that had "messed him over," but the Lord was teaching me that my heart had once fallen victim to the same ploy.

Similar to Craig, I realized my knowledge of right and wrong mostly kept my heart focused on the kingdom of God, but my emotions often tempted me to drift back toward priority service to the temporal kingdom. Despite what I knew was biblical, I occasionally felt a strong pull toward whatever most pleased my administrators and co-workers rather than what God's Word has revealed to be His will. The Lord constantly rescued me from my weaknesses and reminded me that the emotional tug-of-war within me was actually Satan tempting me to do what was right in my own eyes.

My weaknesses were similar to Craig's, but he went to the extreme derailment of rebelling against both the temporal kingdom and the kingdom of God. This double disregard for and rebellion against all authority is precisely the weakness that lands a lot of inmates on death row.

I recall a specific example of an inmate I knew quite well. Benjamin (whose name has been changed for privacy) was serving a short sentence and worked as our office orderly. He served us faithfully every day and always exceeded our expectations of him. He was an energetic, dependable worker who maintained a pleasant attitude and was truly a joy to have around. I knew him for years, had tremendous respect for him, and really liked him a lot. I never knew if Benjamin was a sincere Christian man, but I did know that he was a sincerely good man. He was meek, gentle, and kindhearted and was always smiling and laughing. He was a trustee and he never violated that trust. He seemed to be the best example of a convicted inmate who had learned his lesson and was now submitted to the authority of both kingdoms. When he was paroled, we were all happy for him, but we were seriously going to miss him. Shortly after God had delivered Benjamin from prison and blessed him with freedom, however, the allurements of the world distracted him from respect for and submission to both kingdoms. He was not even out of prison eight months before he and an accomplice shot and killed a Dallas police officer who had caught them committing a crime.

A few years later, strapped to the death gurney with an IV line in his arm, the warden asked Benjamin if he had any last words. He turned his head to look at me and just stared into my eyes. He was not sad or nervous about dying; rather, he was totally humiliated to be in this position in front of "his friends." With a look of heavy embarrassment and shame, he looked away and never said a word. He just shook his head with disgusted disappointment in himself, and then he departed this life.

The good news is that when any of us fail to learn the life lessons God gives us or we fall because of forgetting Him or rebelling against His kingdom agenda, we do not have to die in defeat. The apostle Peter loved and served the Lord with all of his heart. He saw and witnessed firsthand Jesus Himself ushering in the kingdom of God with His perfect life, death on the cross, resurrection from the grave, and establishment of His Church. Yet, when distracted by the world, he often forgot and fell. When you and I are distracted and fall, we can repent and return to God as Peter did, and we will also be forgiven, healed, and restored just as he was. Unfortunately, however, we usually suffer painful consequences for our wayward choices and have to learn some lessons the hard way.

Just as Benjamin was embarrassed before us, I have found myself embarrassed before God as I have knelt before Him in repentance over and over again. It is so humbling to realize how quickly and easily I can be distracted and weakened.

☒ Fill Your Tank with Prayer

The second antidistraction strategy was *beginning each day in prayer.*

Every hour of every day in the penitentiary, Satan tried to empty my tank, so I absolutely had to start each day by filling my tank with Jesus in prayer. The disciplined, daily habit of humbly kneeling before God in total dependence on Him before I did anything else at the start of a day always resulted in my protection. Conversely, I always found that my toughest days and hardest struggles were when I had let something rob me of starting my day in prayer. What a piercing reminder of what I really amount to without Him!

God helped me develop this discipline by listening to the testimony of a friend from my home church who answered the call to teach God's Word to women. Donna Pyle is a Bible study teacher who vulnerably tells women how she is still tempted by the enemy. She admittedly reveals that if she did not start each day in prayer, she would fall. It is clearly visible and obvious that she is consumed with the pursuit of God and loves Him with all of her heart. Upon being questioned about how she ever fell so deeply in love with Jesus, however, she answered that she had to. She explained that if she had not, her natural sinful nature, which she knows all too well, would carry her back to the lifestyle she was delivered from in an instant. Donna is quick to testify that the only strength and power within her is the Jesus she clings to.

This testimony from Donna is especially encouraging to me because every once in a while, Satan triggers one of my weaknesses just enough to remind me that the "old me" is buried deep down underneath decades of healing and blessed transformation—BUT—still there. By God's grace, it is quickly recognized and buried again, even deeper. Those reoccurring temptations to resurrect the old me are a sobering reminder that without a fresh anointing of the Holy Spirit each morning I would not be able, on my own strength, to continue my walk with Jesus.

I needed to start each day in prayer not so much because I was appointed to hold death row inmates accountable for their crimes, but because I was appointed to hold myself accountable to represent the kingdom of God properly while serving the earthly kingdom of government.

☒ Prayer Closets

The third antidistraction strategy was utilization of *prayer closets*. One afternoon while I was walking through death row at the Polunsky Unit, I was watching and listening to one of the inmates who had recently received a stay of execution. As he was talking to several other death row inmates, they were all laughing and making fun of the attorneys, politicians, and activists who had just helped him receive his stay. They were joking about how easy it was to pretend to be mentally handicapped and tug on the hearts of people to fight against his execution. His buddies told him that he was "playing those politicians like a bass fiddle." He laughed and said, "I know, but I'll keep feeding it to them as long as they'll keep buying it." As I stood there witnessing all of this, I caught myself being tempted by many emotions that were not even close to seeking God's kingdom first. Instead, I was having a throwback to my darker days of serving the kingdom of the world with reactions to evil worse than the evil itself.

I was again embarrassed before God to realize how quickly my emotions could still lead my heart in the wrong direction. I immediately stopped whatever I was doing, quickly located some place I could utilize as a "prayer closet," and took a long enough break to

- *spend at least a few minutes of quiet time in prayer with God;*
- *read a little bit of God's Word; and*
- *sing praises to the Lord.*

When temptations and distractions left me so emotionally exhausted and frustrated that I didn't feel like doing any of these, right then and there was the most critical time to do so anyway. These emergency prayer closets always put me in the best position to recognize and enjoy God's grace. Beyond simply starting each day in prayer, I found and utilized prayer closets countless times each day and God rescued me from distractions every single time! They were undoubtedly the Lord's prescription for me to seek Him first and thereby successfully navigate the darkness. I always carried a pocket-size New Testament with me everywhere I went in the prison, because I knew I would need it several times every day.

Whenever I found myself struggling between following my will or God's will, prayer wasn't just help for the fight—it was the fight! The Lord always delivered me from the crisis of the immediate distraction I would be praying about, but He was actually giving me something much greater: time spent in His presence. There was no greater joyous, comforting peace than when I was in focused, personal connection with God in private and intimate prayer!

Whenever I slipped into a little broom closet for a quick prayer-and-praise break from a hectic moment of prison turmoil, God transformed that closet into a holy sanctuary and raised me up to an overcoming power that was nothing short of miraculous! The Lord restored my broken spirit many times and in many different ways, but the fastest healing I received were times when I truly praised and worshiped Him despite my circumstances.

Only weeks before ending my career, I was driving across Huntsville solely for the purpose of using my car as a prayer closet. God was faithful to hear and answer my petitions, even from my mobile "closet." I was singing at the top of my lungs, lifted about as high in the Spirit as possible with renewed strength when I realized that only ten minutes earlier I had been struggling with an exceptionally effective attack from Satan. I was emotionally deflated, down in the dumps, and completely buried under some challenges that I had been dwelling on for hours.

What had caused the lengthy emotional valley I was in only moments earlier?

- *Focusing primarily on my authority in my temporal kingdom*

What caused the sudden emotional mountaintop?

- *Focusing primarily on Jesus' authority and His kingdom*

While I was wondering how I ever allowed the condition of my heart to become so distracted from my focus on God, I remembered that I had not utilized a prayer closet of any kind, walked closely with God, or sung His praises in almost two weeks. We had an escape from one of the Huntsville-area units, and I had been on a lengthy manhunt, along with hundreds of other prison employees, searching for this inmate. I was combing the backwoods and trails of East Texas day and night with very little sleep.

All prison duties must be taken seriously, but an escape chase demands ultimate focus. Most crisis situations that correctional employees face are at least contained within the fences of a prison. Even serious staff assaults from the most dangerous wolves within the penitentiary are confined to a known enemy on our own turf. Once an inmate escapes the compound and is loose somewhere out in the free world, however, the dangers are compounded. That person is now capable of having an unlimited amount of weapons and friends helping him or her. An escaped convict on the run is much more dangerous because he is extremely desperate and will often resort to any means necessary to avoid apprehension. The tension rises with every hour of every day an inmate is on the run because it increases his chances of hurting people in the free world. We get tired, but we have to keep the pressure on so that the escapee becomes more exhausted than us and lets his guard down. That strategy worked in this particular case, but it took almost two solid weeks.

My devoted efforts to help apprehend the escaped inmate were honorable and necessary, but I let my focus on my authority take me out of fellowship with the Lord. The manhunt became an all-consuming task that had caused me not only to miss church services during that time but also to neglect prayer, and my soul was malnourished and weakened by losing so much focus on God.

I was embarrassed before God to realize that it only took two weeks for my strong fellowship with the Lord to fall into stagnation. It only took two minutes, however, to climb out of that weakened, vulnerable state and leap back into the full joy of the Lord and enabling power of the Holy Spirit when I returned to prayer and praise. I was thankful for the quick recovery, but I was also extremely disappointed in myself for failing to seek His face for so long. This experience of giving one-hundred percent of my heart, mind, soul, and strength to serve the secular kingdom with my temporal authority and zero percent to the One who established and gave me my authority really convicted me to the deepest core of my soul. I even found myself rethinking my ability to ever become any kind of a credible ministry worker in a second career.

My twenty-year quest to know God's will in the most disturbing aspects of capital punishment ultimately led me to this very destination—the blessing of a disciplined habit of a daily nearness to God. My search for the answers to punitive justice problems ultimately helped me find the answer to all problems. Although it required endless lessons of humbling, I progressively learned that constantly seeking first the kingdom of God is what matters most to Him. At the end of a long career filled with innumerable life lessons, I was still learning the most important one.

On my final day with the Texas Department of Criminal Justice I was in a surreal mode of thanksgiving and amazement over how many ways I experienced God at work in that place. As I walked out of the prison for the last time and stepped off of the porch and out into the street, I looked up to heaven and smiled. I was thankful that God enabled me to end well and represent Him well in one of the most challenging callings on earth. I was thankful that my governmental responsibility to wield the sword of restraint and punishment was over. Never again would I be an appointed agent of God's wrath. I had ended my commissioned duty to serve the kingdom of civil government. I would still be living simultaneously in the two kingdoms, but only serving in one.

As I walked across the street, it dawned on me that I was taking the same walk away from the prison as all of the hundreds of inmates that we released each day. In the same way that they walk away mentally preparing themselves for their new life out in the free world, I, too, was imagining the transition as I left this career behind and embraced another. I knew that I was walking away from a wolf pen that was still overflowing with misery and suffering. What I never dreamed, however, was how applicable all of my prison experiences would be in the next chapter of life God had prepared for me.

CHAPTER 14

Shaped by the Sword of the Spirit

After retiring from the penitentiary, I went to work for a friend while I counseled with my pastors and weighed the different seminary and ministry career path options. The friend I worked for was the president of a huge commercial janitorial business, and I became a customer relations and operational troubleshooter for him. As I performed my roll of helping to resolve challenges incurred by his operations managers, I soon realized that this was a good fit for me in this season of my life.

Some of our customers were occasionally violently angry and physically confrontational over some service complaint. I had only been on this job a few weeks when I found myself in the familiar position of having people curse and threaten me while jabbing a confrontational finger in my face. Because of how God had shaped my heart in prison, I was enabled to be gentle as a dove (not twist their arm behind their back and apply handcuffs) yet wise as a serpent (discuss viable solutions rather than feel intimidated). My caring disposition, along with zero alarm over customers' best efforts to be intimidating, caught them off guard, quenched their flaming anger, and became the beginning of strong, trusted relationships.

When I was sharing some of those episodes with my pastor one day, I told him that my prison experiences were actually helpful in my business-relations job, but they probably wouldn't be of much help in church ministry work. He quickly said, "You would be surprised!" He smiled as he explained that my abilities would serve me well in dealing with upset church members more than I realized.

While working in that industry, God continued to humble me by exposing me to the fascinating world of the janitorial employees. The more I came to know these people, the more I realized that most of them had a heart and character that put mine to shame. These people had the lowest paying jobs that required the dirtiest, most demeaning tasks, but I would regularly observe them joyfully singing Christian praise and worship songs while they worked with all their might to scrub toilets and clean up filthy messes.

In my evening inspections I regularly observed successful, professional people working in their executive suites late into the night with very obvious displays of disgruntled frustrations, anger, and stress while my janitorial workers cheerfully emptied their trash cans, mopped their floors, and scrubbed their coffee cups. What a contrast. The professionals who seemed to have everything were miserable, while the cleaners who seemed to have nothing were peaceful and contented. God used that season of working in that position to enable me to understand more about the different cultural contexts in which I would inevitably be trying to serve as pastor.

☒ The Cost of Happiness

One evening I observed one of my project managers crying in her office. I asked her what was troubling her. She explained a situation that has stirred my soul ever since. She shared with me how she had come to the United States from Central America many years ago. She explained that her life back in Honduras had been a very meager existence with virtually no money or possessions, yet it was a good, happy life. Back in Honduras, she had her family, her community, and her church. Her mind seemed to go back in time as she smiled and said that everyone respected one another, helped one another, and worshiped God together.

She then sighed as she explained how some of her friends told her that they were leaving and going to the United States. They told her that if she would go with them, they would all some day have many wonderful things in America such as televisions, cars, and even their own home. She started out as a minimum-wage toilet cleaner and worked her way up to being a supervisor and eventually a project manager. She then looked at me and said that she now has everything her friends told her she could have . . . and even more. She paused in silence for a moment, then continued her story by saying that she would give it all away in a heartbeat if she could have nothing . . . and be happy again.

Tears then came to her eyes as she dropped her head and looked down at the floor in defeat. She described how she worked two or three jobs at a time for many years to have the lifestyle she now enjoys. She worked so hard that she had no time for her family, friends, or church. She provided well for her children but at the expense of them not knowing her or God. They now run with the wrong crowd and are in constant trouble. She summarized her dilemma by stating that she would give it all away if she could have a relationship with her family and her God again.

I was able to console and counsel her some that day. God used that experience to paint a picture that has helped me to understand the dilemma of people from every culture and economic class. Most of all, that experience helped me to know myself better. Since that evening, I forgot about my driving desire to completely finance my seminary experience before I started. The total devotion to seminary studies would put my family in a situation of smaller income and different lifestyle than we were accustomed to, but the lesson I learned from my project manager made me desire and trust God more than any thoughts for financial or material comfort.

$\boxed{X}$ God Is Amazing

The last hurdle I needed to jump over before diving into seminary was a consideration of time. I sat in my pastor's office one day to boldly confront him with the question that had become a major concern. After a little bit of small talk and pleasantries, I looked him right in the eye and became very somber and serious. I told him that I had been watching him closer and closer for the last several years. I told him that I had observed him counseling many different people every day, rushing to hospitals, attending meetings, preparing for sermons, preparing for Bible studies, and working late into the night more often than not. I told him, "I know you." I told him how I had observed that his time with his family was constantly interrupted with the need to resolve some church member's crisis. I said, "I see you pouring yourself into everyone else, all day, every day." I finally told him, "You don't have a life!"

A large smile grew on his face. His smile was not pushed out in a condescending way, but in a comforting, reassuring way. He then leaned over and put his hand on my shoulder. With beaming confidence and excitement, he told me, "For a pastor who loves his God and his church, this *is* your life."

He explained that everything he has given up to make time for all of the demands of serving the flock was a great trade-off. God somehow gives him plenty of time for his family and for everything that really matters. He explained that to answer the call, you have to want this life more than any other life. Interruptions to family life have taught him and his family to have a heart that appreciates those interruptions as opportunities from God to share their lives rather than live for self.

That explanation penetrated to the center of my soul. His answer with his obvious joy and excitement became contagiously exhilarating. I suddenly wanted to have his life that I had thought was no life at all. I actually became eager to trade some good things for the better things of the kingdom of God.

By the completion of the four-year journey through Concordia Seminary in St. Louis, I knew that I needed every minute of the soul-shaping studies and experiences God put me through. The seminary's Specific Ministry Program (SMP) enabled me to be called to full-time ministry in my home congregation of Salem Lutheran Church in Tomball, Texas, and to serve them as Care Ministry pastor.

God is amazing. A wayward sheep proud and committed to being cold, callous, and condemning was transformed to be a compassionate and caring shepherd. What a testimony of the truth of Proverbs 16:9: "The heart of man plans his way, but the LORD establishes his steps."

Only by the grace of God was I

- *spared from becoming a wolf in prison;*
- *forgiven and adopted as a sheep of His flock;*
- *redeemed and rebuilt after making a wreck of my life;*
- *enabled to have ears to recognize His voice in His Word;*
- *given a renewed heart when appointed to wield the sword of the state; and*
- *humbled by intense struggle before being ordained to wield the sword of the Spirit.*

The Lord was with me when I walked through the valley of the shadow of death row. He was beside me while in seminary as I tried to learn proper theology through damaged filters. Both journeys required going deep into God's Word. My character was shaped, honed, polished, and humbled by God's design. He saw fit to teach amazing life lessons from death row. He then allowed me to sit at the feet of dozens of brilliant seminary professors so that I could interpret those lessons through the lens of professional exegetes.

Although just a beginner compared to some pastors and scholars, I appreciated learning how to become an exegete of Scripture. Since being ordained and called to full-time ministry, I am extremely thankful for the lessons on how to wield the sword of the Spirit effectively and responsibly.

Serving God in a church of thousands presents a myriad of different opportunities to share His Word. My biggest responsibility is to visit hospitals, nursing homes, and hospice patients. It is amazing that I spent so much time in prison helping people who were suffering and/or about to die. In the pastoral ministry, I am in a different atmosphere yet in a very similar situation.

☒ Submit to Your Savior

Although retired from serving in the penitentiary, being a Care Ministry pastor has sent me back into the prisons regularly to visit the incarcerated children of families in my congregation. The Lord has answered my prayers to be able to go deeper in my service to inmates and their families in ways that would never be possible for an active prison employee.

In one-on-one counseling with inmates, as well as group talks to high school students and church youth groups, I use stories of prison experiences as applications of messages from God's Word. The Lord has used these talks to penetrate stubborn, stony hearts. He has enabled some wayward young sheep to be killed by the conviction of His Law and made alive again by the balm of His Gospel.

A sad but effective lesson I share is about inmate Smith (not his real name). This young man came to prison when he was only eighteen years old. He was a brilliant, respectable high school student. He attended church regularly and was very active in his youth group. His use of alcohol was infrequent, but one night he was both drinking and driving with the wrong crowd when he accidentally swerved off the road and up onto a sidewalk. He struck several people with his vehicle, killing one and crippling others. Mothers Against Drunk

Drivers (MADD) lobbied for a stiff penalty, and he was sentenced to forty years.

This somber situation helps students understand that they don't have to be a hardened criminal to fall prey to Satan's temptations and ruin their lives. It is a sobering jolt for them to hear me explain that this inmate will be my age by the time he leaves prison. It creates a "scared straight" moment when I explain that he may not ever leave prison alive because he is frequently raped there, which has made him a serious suicide risk.

I rarely have trouble keeping students' attention when I explain that they can count on their parents and Jesus to love and forgive them when they make bad decisions and dumb mistakes, but judges and juries will not. They get the blunt message that ethnic and social class discrimination can unfortunately be sickeningly real in courtrooms. Therefore, the only way to be sure to avoid such mistreatment is to stay out of the courtroom by obediently submitting to their Savior who loves them, so they don't have to submit to the judgment and sentencing of those who don't!

I also address the teachers, youth group leaders, and chaperones, explaining that we adults must also obediently submit to our Savior. Unless there is a blatant example of a government leader commanding us to sin, we must support them. In such cases, the Bible tells us that we must obey God rather then men (Acts 5:29). Such abuse of power has indeed happened numerous times in history but cannot be used as an excuse for blanket disrespect for those God has ordained to wield the sword of the state. God's Word commands that we render unto Caesar what is Caesar's (Matthew 22:21). Satan lies to us adults to deceive us into feeling justified in rebelling against God's appointed protectors of His sheep. All of us must know and obey God's Word to do His will.

Whether I am in prisons, hospitals, nursing homes, or at hospice bedsides, each visit is a uniquely personal situation. It's amazing how there is always some portion of God's Word I have recently read that turns out to be the perfect words of comfort or counsel for that specific situation. Constant and careful exegesis of Scripture aids my recognition of God's voice speaking to me through His Word that I have guarded in my heart for such times. But the words that heal, console, and bless the most powerfully are always His, not mine.

☒ Jesus Is the Answer

Since laying down the sword of the state and picking up the sword of the Spirit, it has amazed me how those two worlds can be so similar. In each calling, I served people who were grieving, suffering, and/or dying. The pain and suffering of the free-world people seems every bit as crushing as those in prison.

In both worlds, however, the most striking similarity is the way people react to their crisis predicament. Whether in the hospital or in the execution chamber, those who love and trust Jesus have peace and those who reject Him do not. Believers in Christ are not better people than scoffers, but they are in a better position when it comes to suffering. Both suffer very real and difficult pain, but their reactions are different for a variety of reasons.

- *Scoffers are limited to reason and logic.*
  Believers walk by faith, not by sight.
- *Scoffers blame God and reject Him.*
  Believers trust God and draw closer to Him.
- *Scoffers go through suffering alone.*
  Believers know they are never alone.
- *Scoffers despair because of no hope.*
  Believers hope in divine promises.
- *Scoffers know their loss is final.*
  Believers know their loss is temporary.
- *Scoffers crumble because of no foundation.*
  Believers stand on their solid rock.

- *Scoffers don't fear God but fear everything else.*
  Believers fear God alone.
- *Scoffers cling to their anger.*
  Believers cling to the cross of Christ.

My purpose in showing these predictable differences is not to elevate Christians above suffering but to elevate Christ as the way, the truth, and the life despite our suffering. It was never God's desire for man to know pain, suffering, and death. Man brought all of those consequences into the world when he sinned. When God created the world, there was no violence or murder, and the wolf lived peacefully with the lamb. From the moment man attempted to take control of his own life rather than surrendering control to God, wolves began to steal, kill, and destroy God's sheep.

Even if our pain was caused by no fault of our own, we live in a sin-filled world and the consequences affect everyone. Our country is extremely violent and is one of the world leaders in capital punishment—not so much because of a faulty criminal justice system, but because of our sin and our celebration of sin. Let us not make the costly mistake of blaming or rejecting God when suffering or hardships engulf us; rather, let us grow more dependent on Him. The terrible frequency of capital murder and capital punishment in this country is merely an inevitable and unavoidable symptom of a horribly sin-sick nation.

Sin is the problem.
Jesus is the answer.

There will never be complete justice this side of heaven, because sin inhibits justice. Unfortunately, we are all a part of the problem because everyone has sinned and contributed to the wages of sin in our world. Every person's sin is similar to the original sin of Adam—an attempt to take control of our own lives. The biblical promise of the return of Christ and the reclamation of creation is the only answer to completely overcoming evil and injustice.

God's answer to sin was to provide a way for man's broken relationship with Him to be restored. He gave His only begotten Son, Jesus, to be the perfect sacrificial Lamb that takes away the sin of the world. The Bible promises us that God has accepted the price Jesus paid on the cross as the all-sufficient, once-for-all payment-in-full for our sins. We don't deserve it or earn it; we can only receive it in faith. There is therefore no condemnation for those who receive His free gift of grace in Christ Jesus. Believers are buried with Christ through Baptism into death in order that, just as Christ was raised from the dead through the glory of the Father, we, too, may have a new life.

The ultimate crime is not capital murder; it is a deliberate rejection of God's grace. The ultimate penalty is not capital punishment; rather, it is to be granted the wish to be separated from God. Many Americans who resist the law enforcement powers God gave to earthly governments claim they are merely fighting for the same freedom as our forefathers who signed a declaration of independence from the King of England. In reality, however, what they are actually fighting for is independence from the King of kings.

God saw fit to shape and humble my heart through the strange context of life lessons from death row inmates. Capital punishment is a sad and horrible part of life, but I submit to God's will to give that power to the state. Although we should support those commissioned to restrain evil and protect us, we should also keep an ever cautious and careful eye on government executions, because our hearts should never become comfortable with the practice. In this way, we will all do our part to honor God's provisions for protecting His sheep while loving the wolves.

As you have traveled this journey with me, I hope that you have experienced the love of God reaching out to wolves, to wounded sheep, and to you. I hope you have learned that even though God allows governments to use the sword against human wolves, He still loves them and expects us to do the same. I hope you have discovered that the Lord has given us guidance in His Word on how to control crime, but He is far more concerned about whom we are allowing to control our hearts.

If you have suffered greatly from the loss of a loved one to capital murder or from the loss of a loved one to capital punishment, I am so sorry for your loss and your plight to deal with all that has happened. My prayer is that you would allow God to comfort you and guide the direction of your heart.

If you are not personally afflicted by capital murder or its consequences, please pray for death row inmates, their families, and the families of their victims. Please pray for those who risk their lives daily to protect us from predators, that they be enabled to protect the sheep yet love the wolves.

My prayer is that the Holy Spirit has enabled you to learn the ultimate life lesson that Jesus is *your* way, *your* truth, and *your* life. I pray that you have received God's grace and are a sheep of His flock who will see the reclamation of creation when the wolf dwells peacefully with the lamb once again.

Until then, I pray:

May the God of peace who brought again from the dead our Lord Jesus, the great shepherd of the sheep, by the blood of the eternal covenant, equip you with everything good that you may do His will, working in us that which is pleasing in His sight, through Jesus Christ, to whom be glory forever and ever. Amen. (Hebrews 13:20–21)

ACKNOWLEDGMENTS

God gets all the credit and glory for the redemption and shaping that took place in my life along with the ability to share that experience with others through this book. I am thankful to my wife, Jill, for her patience, help, and support during my career and this writing. Thanks go to the Texas Department of Criminal Justice, Sam Houston State University, the Houston Police Department, the Tomball Police Department, Salem Lutheran Church, Concordia Seminary, and the amazing staff at Concordia Publishing House, especially Laura Lane and Elizabeth Pittman. I am also thankful for the following friends and family who helped me as "writing coaches" by counseling me on how to write my story in a manner that was palatable to readers: Patricia Kym, Doug Dommer, JoAnn Cowan, Carolyn Forsche, Tammy Vankirk-Morrisette, Helen Durham, Olivia Abernethy, Jill Carter, Catherine Weber, and Gus Jacob.